ON THE

CONSERVATION OF SOLAR ENERGY

ON THE

CONSERVATION OF SOLAR ENERGY

A COLLECTION OF PAPERS AND DISCUSSIONS

C. WILLIAM SIEMENS, F.R.S., D.C.L.

GYAN

Published by

Gyan Publishing House
5, Ansari Road
Daryaganj, New Delhi-110002
Phone: 011-47034999, 9811692060
E-mail: books@gyanbooks.com

Distribution Network
gyanbooks.com
India, USA, Canada, UK, Australia, France

ISBN : 978-81-212-9472-0 (PB)
First Published, 1883

2nd Impression 2023

Printed at: Gyan Press, Delhi.

ON THE CONSERVATION OF SOLAR ENERGY
Author:C. WILLIAM SIEMENS

ON THE

CONSERVATION OF SOLAR ENERGY.

ON THE

CONSERVATION OF SOLAR ENERGY

A COLLECTION OF PAPERS AND DISCUSSIONS

BY

C. WILLIAM SIEMENS, F.R.S., D.C.L.

LL.D., PH.D., MEM. INST. C.E.

WITH ILLUSTRATIONS

1883

DEDICATION.

SHERWOOD, TUNBRIDGE WELLS,
April 4th, 1883.

DEAR MR. SPOTTISWOODE,

When, a twelvemonth ago, I ventured to communicate to the Royal Society my hypothesis regarding the Conservation of Solar Energy, I thought it advisable to confine myself to a concise statement of my views, in order to fix the attention of my audience upon the principles of action which I wished to submit for their consideration. That audience, comprising astronomers and physicists more familiar with the intricacies of solar physics than I could pretend to be, would, I thought, prefer the simple statement of my views to an elaboration of proofs, some of which they might possibly have deemed superfluous, and others objectionable in leading their attention away from the simple conception to matters of detail. In the short space of time which has elapsed since the reading of my paper, the amount of positive information regarding solar physics has been greatly augmented. The elaborate report to the American Government regarding the eclipse of 1880 had not appeared at the time I prepared my paper, but has since furnished a striking confirmation of the luminous equatorial extension of the sun which I had represented in a hypothetical diagram; other valuable information has been furnished, by observations in Egypt, of the solar eclipse of last year. The spectroscope, in the hands of Captain Abney and of Professor Langley, has furnished important evidence to the effect that solar rays are absorbed before they reach the outer confines of our atmosphere, pointing to the existence between the two atmospheres of a highly-attenuated medium comprising, according to Captain Abney, hydrocarbons of the ethyle group. The light thrown upon the differential motion of the photosphere by Mr. Carrington has been supplemented by the elaborate series of observations on the motion of sun-spots by Dr. Spoerer of Potsdam, and by very recent communications to the Paris Academy by M. Faye, who, although not admitting my hypothesis of a polar inflow current, has resorted to a polar outflow current in order to explain the photospheric polar retardation, and the cyclonic action to which the appearance and motion of sun-spots are attributable.

While thus encouraged by the accumulation of facts, and further by the approval of friends to follow up the hypothesis, upon which I had ventured, not without careful consideration, I am chiefly indebted to those who have taken opposite views for opportunities to enter upon further explanations and additional investigations regarding the principal conditions upon which the working out of my hypothesis depends. It was necessary to prove, amongst other things, that the temperature of the solar photosphere did not exceed the limits at which the combustion of hydrogen and of hydrocarbons can take place; and here again observed facts converge towards the conclusion that the former estimates fixing that temperature at between 12,000° and 20,000° Centigrade are fallacious, and that the real photospheric temperature does not exceed probably 2,800° C.

The effect of a resisting medium in space, in retarding planetary motion, furnishes another consideration of importance outside the question immediately involved; proof has been brought forward to show that the basis upon which such resistance has generally been calculated is untenable, so that astronomers need no longer insist upon a perfect vacuum in order to account for the diminutive amount of the changes that have taken place in the length of our year since the time of the first astronomical records of eclipses 3,000 years ago.

In putting forward my perhaps somewhat daring hypothesis, I was animated by the feeling that although not prepared certainly to discuss intricate questions of solar physics upon equal terms with some of my hearers, I possessed special advantages in having given a life-long attention to questions of combustion, and to the utilisation of different forms of energy upon a comparatively large scale. This led me to look upon the sun in the light of a vast piece of apparatus, worked upon principles such as could be observed and appreciated at their real value, in terrestrial practice.

The fan-like solar action upon which my hypothesis depends has been well discussed in these pages; and I may say that I have not met with any adverse arguments calculated to shake my conviction in the reality of such an action, provided only that space is filled with matter however much attenuated. The further question whether aqueous vapour and carbon-compounds are capable of being dissociated by solar radiation when so attenuated has been viewed favourably as regards my hypothesis by eminent chemists; and I need only refer the reader to the concluding Appendix taken from Professor Liveing as setting forth the accepted views regarding the influence of attenuation upon dissociation; but I am aware some eminent physicists entertain a doubt of the sufficiency of the avowedly incomplete experimental proof which I brought forward in my original paper. I was in hopes that others would have taken up this experimental inquiry, but in default of such aid I have pursued the subject in my own way, and hope shortly to embody the results in a separate communication. Suffice it for present purposes to say that although the quantitative proof is necessarily very difficult, considering the extremely small amount of matter present in a tube filled with highly-attenuated vapour, yet the results of observation are decidedly corroborative of the action which I supposed to take place.

But supposing that no such dissociation at the expense of solar radiation does take place, we shall find ourselves between two difficulties, which have been touched upon only very lightly in this controversy and elsewhere, but which involve, nevertheless, a question of vast importance to the maintenance of a thermal condition of the universe. If space is filled with vapour we shall surely have absorption of solar energy, resulting, unless chemical action be admitted, in thermal effect, thus raising the highly-attenuated gases gradually but surely up to the solar temperature; for, although a boundless space filled with attenuated matter has an infinite capacity for heat, the space comprised between thousands of visible stars—being all Suns like our own—constitutes, in a measure, an interior region which could not remain permanently at a temperature not exceeding probably 100° on the absolute scale. If, on the contrary, we hold with M. Hirn that a perfectly vacuous space can alone satisfy the astronomer, we shall have to admit an expenditure of all but perhaps the millionth part of the energy of the world without conceivable result, an idea which appears to me as much opposed to the modern conception of conservation of energy as the converse case of perpetual motion.

I was much struck with the impartiality with which you

made allusion to my paper in your opening address to the Royal Society in November last, when you expressed yourself as follows: "Upon the questions therein raised the last word has been by no means said; and whether the theory be ultimately established, or whether, like a phœnix, it shall hereafter give rise to some other outcome from its own ashes, it will ever be remembered as having set many active minds at work, and will always have a place in the history of solar physics."

While cordially accepting the position you thus assign to the question at issue, I have been induced by the advice of several friends to combine in a small volume all the discussion of a serious nature which has publicly appeared (chiefly in the pages of *Nature* and in the *Comptes Rendus* of the French Academy of Sciences), in order to prevent rediscussion of the same points, and to put those interested in the question in possession of the arguments that have been used, which would not otherwise be generally accessible.

All things considered, I have every reason to be satisfied with the interest that has been taken in the question I have ventured to bring forward, and I gladly accept the permission, you kindly gave me, of dedicating these pages to you, which I do as a token of that personal regard

With which I remain,

DEAR MR. SPOTTISWOODE,

Yours very sincerely,

C. WILLIAM SIEMENS.

WILLIAM SPOTTISWOODE, ESQ., M.A., D.C.L., &c., &c.,
President of the Royal Society.

CONTENTS.

APPENDIX.

ANALYSIS OF SUBJECTS.

ON THE CONSERVATION OF SOLAR ENERGY.

Enormous amount of heat radiated, p. 1.—Small quantity intercepted. No diminution of solar temperature. Continuance of solar heat accounted for by Helmholtz through shrinkage, p. 2.—Examination of this hypothesis. Fluid supposed in "critical" condition. Convection currents active both in gaseous atmosphere and fluid ocean below, p. 3.—Comparison with steam boiler, p. 4.—Sun spots occur only in two belts between equator and poles, p. 5.—Explained by currents from poles to equator causing cyclones. Convection currents insufficient to account for amount of heat lost by radiation.

Hypothesis that radiant energy is arrested in space and brought back to Sun in another form, p. 6.—Space assumed to contain highly-rarefied gaseous matter. Each planet has its atmosphere. Grove, Humboldt, Zoellner, Mattieu Williams, and also Sir Isaac Newton, have assumed matter in space, p. 7.—(History of Newton's paper), p. 8.—The occluded gases in meteorolites, and spectrum analysis, favour this view, p. 9; but want of retardation of planetary motion opposes it; consideration of this difficulty.

Why the Sun has an outer atmosphere of the light gases, p. 10.—Mairan and La Place on zodiacal light. Solar fan-action described, p. 11.

Dissociation of matter in space by solar heat energy. Bunsen and Sainte Claire Deville on dissociation at high temperature.

Dissociation in leaf-cells of plants at ordinary temperature, p. 12.

The Author's experiments on dissociation in vacuum tubes at a pressure of $\frac{1}{1800}$ atmosphere, p. 13.—Professor Stokes's discovery that ultra-violet rays are absorbed by clear glass. Hence dissociation in space likely to be more active than in vacuum tubes, p. 14.—Fan-like action draws dissociated gases in at poles, and after combustion, it throws them out at the equatorial regions into space.

Professor Piazzi Smyth finds that vacuum tubes containing attenuated vapours become in time hydrogen tubes, p. 15.—Professor Storey and Mr. Meldola have found oxygen in outer solar atmosphere.

Calculation that 8 lbs. of gas, developing 2,100 heat units per pound, flowing at the rate of 100 ft. per second, per sq. ft. of solar heat-receiving surface, would suffice to account for the radiation of heat from the Sun, p. 16.

Comparison of diagram of ideal corona, with real corona photographed by Professor Langley in America, when the Sun was eclipsed on 11th January 1880, p. 17.

Solar absorption spectra favour the view of the existence of gases in space; the metallic vapours in Sun supposed to form a lower atmosphere not participating in fan-action, which is only feasible if density of the inflowing is at equal distance equal to that of the outflowing current; denser vapours may be blown out by explosions and carried away into space to form cosmic dust, p. 18.

Variations in solar heat may be due to variations in condition of gaseous matter in space. Zodiacal light may be due to particles of dust emitting light reflected from the Sun, or to electrical tension similar to that observed by Dr. Werner Siemens on the Chiops Pyramid in Egypt. Other electrical considerations, p. 19.

Outflow from Sun may have caused the large amount of carbonic acid found in the enormous beds of limestone on the earth, p. 20.

Considerations with regard to comets; the nucleus an aggregation of stones; gases absorbed in space would be driven out with enormously increased volume by heat when the comet is moving in perihelion; the nucleus would emit original light, p. 21.

Fundamental conditions of hypothesis: 1. That gases are present in space. 2. That compound gases, when extremely attenuated, can be dissociated by radiant solar energy. 3. That solar rotation draws in dissociated gases at the Sun's polar surfaces, and ejects them equatorially after combustion into space.

On Electrical Discharges in Vacuum Tubes, and their Relation to Solar Physics.

Dr. De la Rue's large battery of 14,400 cells, 14,832 Volt's electromotive force, gave a current of ·054 Ampère, with a discharge at ·71 inch between terminals, p. 22.

Phenomena of stratified discharge similar to those of electric arc, being a disruptive discharge and not a current; length of spark varies as square of number of cells; imitation of the aurora produced in vacuum tube, p. 23.

Mr. Spottiswoode's experiments prove that the dissymmetry in electrical discharges in vacuum tubes is an essential element in every disruptive discharge, and that the phenomena of stratification are always present; the striæ are actual aggregations of matter, p 24.

The importance of these investigations in connection with solar physics; the light thrown on the subject by the spectroscope, p. 25.

The results of the last eclipse expedition; amongst others that hydrocarbons exist between the Sun and earth; absorption of actinic rays shown to take place in solar atmosphere in Professor Langley's experiments, and between solar and terrestrial atmosphere by Captain Abney, p. 26; material continuity between Sun and earth thus established.

Letter from Mr. Charles Morris to *Nature*.

Accepts fan-like action; thinks space is occupied with matter of great tenuity, p. 27.—Nebular hypothesis of contracted matter in planets and rarefied matter in space, p. 28.—Owing to condensation and rarefaction of gaseous matter, Sun would be hot, space cold, p. 29; Sun's heat would be maintained by condensation of inflowing matter; and the outflow of the products of combustion, at the expense of the rotatory energy of the Sun, p. 30.

Letter from Professor Sterry Hunt to *Nature*.

Reference to views of Sir Wm. Grove, of Mr. Mattieu Williams, and Newton on the subject of matter in space, with quotations from these writers, pp. 31-33.—Considers that as far as the Sun's energy is concerned it would be immaterial whether the matter in space was dissociated or merely heated, p. 34.

C. W. Siemens's Reply.

Material in stellar space is intensely cold; if it be assumed at 100° absolute on the Centigrade scale, with density = $\frac{1}{1000000}$ of an atmosphere, the temperature of the solar photosphere due to adiabatic compression would be 2545° C., or below that of powerful electric arcs, p. 35; if this heat be supplemented by that due to the combustion of combustible gases, the whole of the radiant heat is accounted for, p. 36.

The amount of rotative force required to produce fan-action only that necessary to cover frictional retardation, as the flow of gases, when once established, has only to be changed in direction, p. 37.

Letter from Mr. Archibald to *Nature*.

Objects that the centrifugal force is not adequate to produce fan-action, owing to the large amount of solar gravity, p. 38; thinks the solar atmosphere arranged in layers of relative density around the sun, p. 39.

C. W. Siemens's Reply.

Shows that the centrifugal force need not exceed that of gravitation. Assumes two gaseous particles of equal masses at equal distances from the Sun, one in polar, the other in equatorial plane; if the latter revolve around the Sun, the force of gravitation upon it will diminish, and the inequality of attractive forces upon the two particles will cause polar inflow and equatorial outflow, p. 40.

Letter from Professor Fitzgerald to *Nature*.

Asks—1. Why the gases near the Sun do not become an atmosphere around him? 2. Why the planets have not enormous atmospheres? 3. Why the earth is not deluged with the aqueous vapour passing it on the way to space? 4. Why the stars are visible? p. 41.

C. W. Siemens's Reply.

1. The gases flashing into flame have diminished specific gravity, causing a rebound action, which, combined with acquired motion, and centrifugal impulse from contact with lower atmosphere, constitutes a stream from the poles to the equator, and thence into space. Rotatory motion of the Sun, must cause outflow, p. 42.

2. The atmosphere of each spheroid would be that due to its mass; the moon's would be so small as to be scarcely perceptible by means of optical instruments.

3. The amount of vapour that would condense on the earth would depend on its mean temperature, and the vapour density of the stellar atmosphere surrounding it; the earth would only acquire aqueous vapour if its temperature were lower than that of space, p. 43.

4. The stars may still be visible, notwithstanding selective dissociation in space.

Letter from G. B. S. to *Nature*.

Asks what has become of the energy which was present as heat in the earth and planets? and whether the Sun radiates more heat than required for dissociation of gases in space? p. 44.

C. W. Siemens's Reply.

If the earth's rotatory velocity were formerly higher than now, and its surface sufficiently hot to ignite gases, it would have the power of proportional recuperation, until its temperature fell below that of ignition, when it would cool rapidly until its own radiation of heat into space equalled that received from the Sun, the present state, p. 45.

M. Faye on Dr. Siemens's New Theory of the Sun.

Statement of the hypothesis, p. 46.—A vacuum of $\frac{1}{2000}$ very dense from the astronomer's point of view, it would cause excessive resistance to planetary motion, p. 47, and would add a mass of matter to the solar system 100,000 times as great as that of the Sun, p. 48.

C. W. Siemens's Reply.

The distribution in space is such as to insure statical equilibrium between the forces of expansion and diffusion on the one hand, and of attraction towards the Sun and celestial bodies on the other, p. 49.—Mariotte's law as regards tension probably not of universal application, Crookes's experiments favour this view, p. 50.

The amount of rarefaction, $\frac{1}{2000}$, was that in the vacuum tubes experimented on, and if dissociation took place in these it should *a fortiori* in space where the gases must be much more rarefied. Comets in perihelion were assumed to move in a medium of density not exceeding $\frac{1}{3000}$; the density of space was not fixed in original paper, p. 51.

Reference to Captain Abney's and Professor Langley's spectroscopic investigations, to the results of recent solar eclipses, and Professor Schwedoff's observation of the fall of what appeared to be cosmical hailstones.

Density in space would be a function of the temperature; the lowest observed temperature—63° C., the absolute zero—274° C.; that of space must be between these; Regnault's formula not applicable rigorously; but at −130° C. the density about $\frac{1}{1000000}$. Assuming this density at the distance of Mercury, the area would supply in combustion all the heat the Sun requires to keep up its radiation, p. 52.

M. Hirn on Dr. Siemens's Theory of the Sun.

Thinks that Mr. Langley's experiments point to 20,000° C. as the minimum temperature of the Sun, p. 53; hence argues, that if stellar matter were dissociated, its recombination could only take place at an appreciable distance from the photosphere, and in falling into the Sun it would be again dissociated, and would hence contribute nothing to the continuous reproduction of solar temperature.

The stars must lose a proportion of their light by dissociating matter in space and the lustre of the Sun and stars must diminish in a ratio much more rapid than the inverse square of the distance, p. 54.

As regards the necessary tenuity of gaseous matter in space so as not to oppose planetary movements more than astronomical observations indicate, there must not be more than one kilogramme of matter in seven million millions of cubic metres, and this tenuity must be diminished 10,000 times to prevent our atmosphere from being swept away, p. 55.

The astronomer requires an absolute vacuum of matter, and Mr. Hirn thinks this necessity upsets the materialistic theory, p. 56.

C. W. Siemens's Reply.

Adherence to materialistic theory. Previously computed temperatures of the Sun too high, including M. Hirn's of 20,000° C., p. 57; has estimated this temperature at or below 3,000°. Agreement of views between Professor Langley and himself.

Analysis of Professor Tyndall's experiments on the proportional luminosity of light from electric arc, incandescent wire and gas flame.

Calculation that an arc of temperature of 2,500° C. gives one-fourth of its energy in light; Professor Langley considers one-fourth of the Sun's energy is luminous, p. 58; Dr. Siemens argues that, allowing for absorption, the temperature of the photosphere is probably 2,800° C., and that hence the re-dissociation supposed by M. Hirn does not occur.

As regards the objection of a diminution in the visibility of stars, Dr. Siemens thinks the law of the inverse square of the distance may not hold as regards star light, p. 59; Professor Langley has proved absorption, and the great gaps in his solar spectrum seem to indicate wave-lengths less favourable to the decomposition of vapours, and hence capable of traversing space further than other rays.

As regards mechanical resistance: asks whether M. Hirn, in his calculation, had taken the tangential motion of the planet or the duration of its year into account, p. 60; quotation from Froude as to stream-line theory; want of concordant results as to resistance of solids wholly immersed in fluids, p. 61; recent experiments of Messrs. Fowler and Baker support Mr. Froude's theory that an unbounded elastic fluid simply performs a lateral oscillation in allowing a solid body to pass; these experiments point to a diminution of pressure per unit of surface as the surface increases in dimensions.

Reference to gases in meteorites, to zodiacal light, to equatorial extension observed in eclipse in America, to researches of Captain Abney, p. 62, and to Carrington's work on Sun-spots. The retardation in the motion of Sun-spots due to matter flowing in at the polar surfaces, passing on to the equator, and thence into space, p. 63.

A Note from M. Faye on a Letter of M. Spoerer.

The centrifugal force of the sun being $\frac{1}{18000}$ of solar gravity, not competent to throw matter into space, p. 64.

As regards the motion of Sun-spots, the observations of Langier, Carrington, and M. Spoerer, show that the displacement of the spots in latitude is small, that those remote from the equator tend towards and not away from the poles, p. 65. This M. Faye considers is opposed to Dr. Siemens's hypothesis of motion in the other direction; his own observations are to the effect that the motion of the larger spots in latitude is oscillatory, p. 66.

If M. Faye could harmonize the results of observation with the hypothesis of a current from the pole to the solar equator, he would be inclined to accept that hypothesis, p. 67.

A Reply to Dr. Siemens by M. Hirn.

Arguing from Mr. Langley's experiments M. Hirn thinks 20,000° C. is probably within the limit of the temperature of the Sun, as for equal surfaces of radiation the radiation of the Sun is eighty-seven times that from steel in fusion at a temperature of 2,000° C., p. 68.

The experiments of Clausius prove that the temperature in the focus of a perfect concave mirror is always below that of the radiating surface, and as with small mirrors platinum has been melted and the diamond ignited, he argues that as $\frac{9}{10}$ths of the disposable solar heat and light is lost, a number is arrived at much larger than 2,000° C. as the temperature of the Sun, p. 69.

As regards the resistance of fluids, M. Hirn thinks that a fluid which offers no resistance to bodies moving in it is purely hypothetical, that the combustion of shooting stars in a medium which he places at $\frac{1}{10000000}$ of an atmosphere proves high resistance, and finishes by placing the tenuity of gaseous matter at the figure in his previous letter, p. 70.

C. W. Siemens's Reply to MM. Faye and Hirn.

Statement of M. Faye's objections, p. 71. By means of a hypothetical bent tube extending from the Sun in the polar and equatorial directions, it is shown how, if the equatorial branch is supposed to revolve, the matter within it must become lighter and cause a continuous flow into the polar tube, p. 72, the power necessary to maintain the current being derived from solar rotation, p. 73.

Analogous but inverse conditions on the earth to the solar spots, in the form of an equatorial or trade-wind current giving rise in our latitudes to cyclones, p. 74; cause of the deviation of the Sun-spots in latitude is the less resistance in the polar direction, p. 75.

Statement of M. Hirn's objections. Acceptance of Mr. Langley's conclusions that the solar temperature is above 1,800° C., and that the radiation from the Sun is 100 times greater than that from melted platinum, but that this high radiation does not prove any particular temperature in excess of his minimum, p. 76.—Sir William Thomson accepts 3,000° C. as the probable temperature of the Sun, p. 77.

The Author's experiments with parabolic reflector focussing the Sun's rays upon burning gas proved a retardation of the combustion. Reference to the regenerative gas furnace, to partial dissociation within it, and to the radiation from the hot sides and the incandescent gas respectively. Experiments with electric furnaces, p. 78.

With matter as attenuated as M. Hirn calculates it, if at the distance of Neptune or Uranus it would suffice for the purposes of the hypothesis.

As regards resistance of a medium to a large body moving in it, it appears that this is likely to be found proportional to the circumferential development rather than the area of the body, p. 79.

Observations by M. Faye.

M. Faye agrees that the hypothetical tube assumed by the Author would be a means of supplying the gases to the Sun, but adds that the medium must revolve as if rigidly connected with the Sun, p. 80.

The Author answers in a footnote that the matter would enter the polar branch irrespective of any initial motion of the arm, and would he delivered equatorially with the motion imparted to it by the tube, p. 81.

M. Faye's Reply to Two Objections of Mr. Young's against the Cyclonic Theory of Sun-Spots.

Explains that the edges of the Sun-spots do not appear torn and distorted, because it is the upper edge that is visible where the motion is slow and regular, whereas deep down the motion is very violent, p. 82; in terrestrial tornadoes the violent motion is felt on the earth, whilst the summit is hidden in clouds, p. 83; a velocity of 2° per day in the visible motion of the Sun-spot may mean 30,000° a day below in the deep, black, central portion, p. 84.

Summary of reply to Mr. Young's objections, pp. 85-87.

APPENDIX.

The Electric Furnace.

Short description of furnace, p. 91.—Abstract of experiments on wrought iron, p. 92; steel, p. 93; diagram of electric furnace; white iron, cast iron, siliceous pig iron, p. 94; nickel, copper, p. 95; platinum, and tungsten, p. 96.—Remarks on the experiments, p. 97.

Sunlight and Skylight at High Altitudes, by Captain Abney, and Remarks by Mr. Langley.

Captain Abney's observations at high altitude show skies nearly black by comparison with bright objects projected against them; at 8,500 feet of elevation the whole photographic spectrum is represented by a band; the reason of this is the existence of particles of reflecting matter, p. 98; conclusion that hydrocarbons must exist between our atmosphere and the Sun, and it may be in space.

Captain Langley's remarks as to the influence of the selective absorption of our atmosphere and that of the Sun on the spectrum, p. 99; outside the earth's atmosphere the spectrum would be different from the ordinary one, and if the solar atmosphere could be removed a third spectrum would be obtained, p. 100.

Description of the diagrams, showing the distribution of energy in the prismatic spectrum and the normal spectrum, p. 101; prismatic spectrum; extraordinary depression and interruptions of energy, p. 102.

Experiments with the bolometer; labour of determination of wave-lengths, p. 103; normal spectrum, p. 104; main results of observations, an enormous and progressive increase of energy towards the shorter wave-lengths; while all radiations emanate from the solar surface, p. 106, the blue are so much greater in proportion that the proper colour of the Sun as seen in the photosphere is blue, p. 107.

Dissociation of Attenuated Compound Gases, by Professor Liveing.

Statement of the Author's hypothesis; fan-action must be carried on at the expense of the energy of the Sun's rotation, p. 108; the decomposition of compound gases at low pressure not inconsistent with laws of dissociation; absorption of rays by our atmosphere, p. 109; spectrum of comets explained by flame of gas containing hydrocarbons found in meteorites; Dr. Huggins found cyanogen in comets; this may be due to ammonia in hydrocarbon flame, p. 110; interesting when Halley's comet returns, to see whether it shines only by reflected light, or gives again the banded spectrum of hydrocarbons, p. 111.

A COLLECTION

OF

PAPERS AND DISCUSSIONS

ON THE

CONSERVATION OF SOLAR ENERGY.

On the Conservation of Solar Energy. By C. WILLIAM SIEMENS, D.C.L., LL.D., Ph.D., F.R.S., Mem. Inst. C.E. [Received February 20, 1882].

(From the *Proceedings of the Royal Society*, No. 219, 1882.)

Incorporated with this Paper are certain portions of an Article entitled "A New Theory of the Sun," published in the *Nineteenth Century* of April, 1882. The additions are printed in distinctive type.

THE question of the maintenance of Solar Energy is one that has been looked upon with deep interest by astronomers and physicists from the time of La Place downward.

The amount of heat radiated from the Sun has been approximately computed, by the aid of the pyrheliometer of Pouillet, and by the actinometers of Herschel at 18,000,000 of heat units from every square foot of his surface per hour,[1] or, put popularly, as equal to the heat that would

[1] "The classic value by Pouillet is about 1·7 calories. All the determinations made during the last fifty years tend to augment this value; the most

be produced by the perfect combustion every thirty-six hours of a mass of coal (of specific gravity = 1·5) as great as that of our earth.

If the Sun were surrounded by a solid sphere of the radius equal to the mean distance of the Sun from the earth (93,000,000 of miles), the whole of this prodigious amount of heat would be intercepted; but considering that the earth's apparent diameter as seen from the Sun is only seventeen seconds, the earth can intercept only the 2,250-millionth part.

Assuming that the other planetary bodies swell the intercepted heat by ten times this amount, there remains the imposing fact that $\frac{224999999}{225000000}$ of the solar energy is radiated into space, and apparantly lost to the Solar System, and only $\frac{1}{225000000}$ utilised.

Notwithstanding this enormous loss of heat, solar temperature has not diminished sensibly for centuries, if we neglect the periodic changes—apparently connected with the appearance of Sun-spots—which have been observed by Lockyer, Janssen and others, and the question forces itself upon us how this great loss can be sustained without producing an observable diminution of solar temperature even within a human lifetime.

Amongst the ingenious hypotheses intended to account for a continuance of solar heat is that of shrinkage, or gradual reduction of the Sun's volume, suggested by Helmholtz. It may, however, be urged against this theory that the heat so produced would be liberated throughout his mass, and would have to be brought to the surface either by conduction or by convection.

recent, due to Messrs. Soret, Crova, and Violle, lead from 2·2 to 2·5 calories. On account of the large number of observations and very long calculations which they necessitate, I cannot yet assign a definite value, but I find three calories to be about the mean; in other words, deducting the influence of our atmosphere, the solar rays would raise 1 gramme of water 3° Centigrade per minute, for every square centimetre of terrestrial surface normally exposed to their action."—*Observations du Spectre Solaire par M. Langley, Comptes Rendus de l'Académie des Sciences*, vol. xcv. p. 482, 11th Sept. 1882.

This theory as developed by Sir William Thomson has certainly the advantage of accounting for the greatest possible store of heat within the solar mass, because it supposes the latter to consist in the main of a fluid heated to such a degree that if it were relieved at any point of the confining pressure, it would flash into gas of a vastly inferior, but still of an elevated, temperature. It is supposed that such fluid material, or material in the "critical" condition, as Professor Andrews, of Belfast, has named it, is continually transferred to the surface by means of convection currents, that is to say, by currents forming naturally when a fluid substance is cooled at its upper surface, and sinks down after cooling to make room for ascending material at the comparatively higher temperature. It is owing to such convection currents that the temperature of a room is, generally speaking, higher towards the ceiling than towards the floor, and that upon plunging a thermometer into a tank of heated water the surface temperature is found superior to that near the bottom.

These convection currents owe their existence to a preponderance of the cooled descending over the ascending current; but this difference being slight, and the ascending and descending currents intermixing freely, they are, generally speaking, of a sluggish character; hence in all heating apparatus it is found essential to resort either to artificial propulsion or to separating walls between the ascending and the descending currents, in order to give effect to the convective transfer of heat.

In the case of a fluid Sun another difficulty presents itself through the circumstance that the vast liquid interior is enveloped in a gaseous atmosphere, which, although perhaps some thousands of miles in depth, represents a relatively very small store of heat. Convection currents may be supposed active in both the gaseous atmosphere and in the fluid ocean below, but the surface of this fluid must necessarily constitute a barrier between the two convective systems, nor could the convective action of the gaseous atmosphere, that is to say, the simple up and down currents caused by surface refrigeration, be such as to disturb the liquid surface below to any great extent, because each descending current would have had plenty of time to get intermixed with its neighbouring ascending current, and would therefore have reached its least intensity on arriving on the liquid surface.

As regards the liquid, its most favourable condition for heating purposes would be at the critical point, or that at which the slightest diminution of superincumbent pressure would make it flash off into gas; but considering that, by means of conduction and convection, the liquid matter must have assumed in the course of ages a practically uniform temperature to a very considerable depth, it follows that the liquid below the surface, with fluid pressure in addition to that of the superimposed gaseous atmosphere, must be ordinary fluid, the critical condition being essentially confined only to the surface.

Conditions analogous to those here contemplated are met with in a high-pressure steam boiler, with its heated water and dense vapour atmosphere. Suppose the fire below such a boiler be withdrawn, and its roof be exposed to active radiation into space, what, it may be asked, should we observe through a strong pane of glass inserted in the side of the boiler near the liquid surface, lit up by an incandescent electric lamp within? The loss of heat by radiation from the boiler would give rise to convection currents, and partial condensation of the vapour atmosphere; then, if the motion of the water was made visible by means of colouring matter, we should observe convection currents in the fluid mass separate and distinct from those in the gaseous mass; but these convection currents would cause no visible disturbance of the liquid surface, which would present itself to the eye with the smoothness of a mirror. It is only in the event of the steam pressure being suddenly relieved at any point, that a portion of the water would flash into steam, causing a violent upheaval of the liquid.

The dark spots on the Sun appear to indicate commotion of this description, but these are evidently not the result of mere convection currents; if they were, they would

Sir John Herschel's Sun-Spot Belts.

occur indiscriminately over the entire surface of the Sun, whereas telescopic observation has revealed the fact that they do occur almost exclusively in two belts, between the Equator and the polar surfaces on either side, as originally shown by Sir John Herschel. Their occurrence could be satisfactorily explained* if we could suppose the existence of strong lateral currents flowing from the polar surfaces towards the Equator, which lateral currents in the solar atmosphere would cause cyclones extending into a lower and denser atmosphere and consisting probably of metallic vapours; this cyclonic action extending downward would relieve the fluid ocean locally from pressure, and give rise to explosive outbursts of enormous magnitude, projecting the lower substance high above the photosphere, with a velocity measured, according to Lockyer, by a thousand miles a second. It will be seen from what follows how, according to my views, such cyclonic action in those intermediate regions of the Sun would necessarily be produced.

But, supposing that, notwithstanding the difficulties just pointed out, convection currents sufficed to effect a transfer of internal heat to the surface with sufficient rapidity to account for the enormous surface-loss by radiation, we should still be at a loss to account for the heat so dispersed, and should only have the poor satisfaction of knowing that the available store would last longer than might have been expected, whereas the only complete solution of the problem would be furnished by a theory, according to which *the radiant energy which is now supposed to be dissipated into space and irrecoverably lost to our Solar System, could be arrested and brought back in another form to the Sun himself, there to continue the work of solar radiation.*

Some years ago it occurred to me that such a solution of the solar problem might not be beyond the bounds of possibility, and although I cannot claim intimate acquaintance with the intricacies of solar physics, I have watched the progress of this branch of science, and have engaged also in some physical experiments bearing upon the question, all of which have served to strengthen my confidence and ripened in me the determination to submit my views, not without some misgiving, to the touchstone of scientific criticism.

For the purposes of my theory, stellar space is supposed

to be filled with highly rarefied gaseous matter, including probably hydrogen, oxygen, nitrogen, carbon, and their compounds, besides solid materials in the form of dust. If this be the case, each planetary body would attract to itself an atmosphere depending for its density upon its relative attractive importance, and it would not seem unreasonable to suppose that the heavier and less diffusible gases would form the staple of these atmospheres; that, in fact, they would consist mostly of nitrogen, oxygen, and carbonic anhydride, whilst hydrogen and its compounds would predominate in space.

But the planetary system, as a whole, would exercise an attractive influence upon the gaseous matter diffused through space, and would therefore be enveloped in an atmosphere, holding an intermediate position between the individual planetary atmospheres and the extremely rarefied atmosphere of stellar space.

In support of this view it may be urged, that in following out the molecular theory of gases as laid down by Clausius, Clerk Maxwell, and Sir William Thomson, it would be difficult to assign a limit to a gaseous atmosphere in space[1] and further, that some writers, among whom I will here mention only Grove, Humboldt, Zoellner, and Mattieu Williams, have boldly asserted the existence of matter occupying all space and accomplishing important functions; moreover, Newton himself, as Dr. Sterry Hunt tells us in an interesting paper which has only just reached me, has expressed views in favour of such an assumption.

The history of Newton's paper is remarkable and very suggestive. It was read before the Royal Society on the 9th and 16th of December, 1675, and remained

[1] Except in assuming that the point of absolute zero is reached by adiabatic expansion upward. Regarding this question much valuable information will be found in the six treatises by Dr. A. Ritter, 1879, entitled, *Anwendung der Mechanischcn Waermetheorie auf Kosmologische Probleme,* in which he shows that our atmosphere should, in obedience to the laws of adiabatic expansion, be limited to a height of 40 kilometers, whereas Schiepperelli has observed at the elevation of 200 kilometers an atmosphere of sufficient density to ignite meteorolites by frictional resistance.

unpublished until 1757, when it was printed by Birch, the then secretary, in the third volume of his *History of the Royal Society*, but received no attention; in 1846 it was published in the *Philosophical Magazine* at the suggestion of Harcourt, but was again disregarded; and now, once more, only a few months since, an astronomer on the other side of the Atlantic brings back to the birthplace of Newton his forgotten and almost despised work of 200 years ago.[1]

If at the time referred to, chemistry had been understood as it now is, and if Newton had been armed moreover with that most wonderful of all modern scientific instruments, the spectroscope, the direct outcome of his own prismatic analysis of light, there appears to be no doubt that the author of the laws of gravitation would have so developed his thoughts upon solar fuel, that they would have taken the form rather of a scientific discovery than of a mere speculation.

Further than this, we have the facts that meteorolites, whose flight through stellar, or at all events through interplanetary space, is suddenly arrested by being brought into

[1] Newton in his Hypothesis imagines "an ethereal medium much of the same constitution with air, but far rarer, subtler, and more elastic." "But it is not to be supposed that this medium is one uniform matter, but composed partly of the main phlegmatic body of ether, partly of other various ethereal spirits, much after the manner that air is compounded of the phlegmatic body of air intermixed with various vapours and exhalations." Newton further suggests in his Hypothesis that this complex spirit or ether, which by its elasticity is extended throughout all space, is in continual movement and interchange. "For Nature is a perpetual circulatory worker, generating fluids out of solids, and solids out of fluids; fixed things out of volatile, and volatile out of fixed; subtile out of gross, and gross out of subtile; some things to ascend and make the upper terrestrial juices, rivers, and the atmosphere, and by consequence others to descend for a requital to the former. And as the earth, so perhaps may the Sun imbibe this spirit copiously, to conserve his shining, and keep the planets from receding farther from him; and they that will may also suppose that this spirit affords or carries with it thither the solary fuel and material principle of life, and that the vast ethereal spaces between us and the stars are for a sufficient repository for this food of the Sun and planets." "Thus, perhaps, may all things be originated from ether."

collision with our earth, are known to contain as much as six times their own volume of gases taken at atmospheric pressure; Dr. Flight has only very recently communicated to the Royal Society the analysis of the occluded gases of one of these meteorolites taken immediately after the descent as follows:—

CO_2	0·12
CO	31·88
H	45·79
CH_4	4·55
N	17·66
	100·00

It appears surprising that there was no aqueous vapour,[1] considering there was much hydrogen and oxygen in combination with carbon, but perhaps the vapour escaped observation, or was expelled to a greater extent than the other gases by external heat when the meteorolite passed through our atmosphere. Opinions concur that the gases found occluded in meteorolites cannot be supposed to have entered into their composition during the very short period of traversing our atmosphere, but if any doubt should exist on this head, it ought to be set at rest by the fact that the gas principally occluded is hydrogen, which is not contained in our atmosphere in any appreciable quantity.

Further proof of the fact that stellar space is filled with gaseous matter is furnished by spectrum analysis, and it appears from recent investigation, by Dr. Huggins and others, that the nucleus of a comet contains very much the same gases found occluded in meteorolites, including "carbon, hydrogen, nitrogen, and probably oxygen," whilst, according to the views set forth by Dewar and Liveing, it also contains nitrogenous compounds such as cyanogen.

[1] My attention has lately been directed to an article, by Dr. Mohr, in Liebig's *Annalen*, vol. clxxix., proving 1·149 per cent. of water in a meteorite that fell at Parnella in India.

Adversely to the assumption that interplanetary space is filled with gases, it is urged that the presence of ordinary matter would cause sensible retardation of planetary motion, such as must have made itself felt before this; but assuming that the matter filling space is an almost perfect fluid not limited by border surfaces, it can be shown on purely mechanical grounds, that the retardation by friction through such highly attenuated medium would be very slight indeed, even at planetary velocities.[1]

But it may be contended that, if the views here advocated regarding the distribution of gases were true, the Sun should draw to himself the bulk of the least diffusible, and therefore the heaviest gases, such as carbonic anhydride, carbonic oxide, oxygen and nitrogen, whereas spectrum analysis has proved on the contrary a prevalence of hydrogen in the photosphere.

In explanation of this seeming anomaly, it can be shown in the first place, that the temperature of the Sun is so high, that such compound gases as carbonic anhydride and carbonic oxide, could not exist within him; it has been contended, indeed, by Mr. Lockyer, that none of the metalloids exist at these temperatures, although as regards oxygen, Dr. Draper asserts its presence in the solar photosphere. There must be regions, however, outside that thermal limit, where their existence would not be jeopardised by heat, and here great accumulation of those comparatively heavy gases that constitute our atmosphere would probably take place, were it not for a certain counterbalancing action.

I here approach a point of principal importance in my argument, upon the proof of which my further conclusions must depend.

The Sun completes one revolution on his axis in 25 days, and his diameter being taken at 882,000 miles, it follows that the tangential velocity amounts to 1·25 miles per second, or to 4·41 times the tangential velocity of our earth. This high rotative velocity of the Sun must cause an

[1] See reply to Messrs. Faye and Hirn, pp. 61, 62 and 79.

equatorial rise of the solar atmosphere to which Mairan, in 1731, attributed the appearance of the zodiacal light. La Place rejected this explanation on the ground that the zodiacal light extended to a distance from the Sun exceeding our own distance, whereas the equatorial rise of the solar atmosphere due to his rotation could not exceed $\frac{9}{20}$ths of the distance of Mercury. But it must be remembered that La Place based his calculation upon the hypothesis of an empty stellar space (filled only with an ether not subject to the laws of gravitation), and that the result of solar rotation would be widely different, if it was supposed to take place within a medium of unbounded extension. In this case pressure would be balanced all round, and the Sun would act mechanically upon the floating matter surrounding him in the manner of a fan, drawing it towards himself upon the polar surfaces, and projecting it outward in a continuous disk-like stream. By this fan action, hydrogen, hydrocarbons, and oxygen, are supposed to be drawn in enormous quantities toward the polar surfaces of the Sun; during their gradual approach, they will pass from their condition of extreme attenuation and extreme cold, to that of compression, accompanied with rise of temperature, until on approaching the photosphere, they burst into flame, giving rise to a great development of heat, and a temperature commensurate with their point of dissociation at the photospheric density. The result of their combustion will be aqueous vapour and carbonic anhydride or oxide according to the sufficiency or the insufficiency of oxygen present to complete the combustion, *and these products of combustion in yielding to the influence of propulsive force will flow toward the solar equator, and be thence projected into space.*[1]

The next question for consideration is: What would become of these products of combustion when thus rendered back into space? Apparently they would gradually change the condition of stellar material, rendering it more and more neutral, but I venture to suggest the possibility, nay, the probability, *that solar radiation would, under these circum-*

[1] See replies to Messrs. Archibald and Faye, pp. 40, 41, and 72, 73.

stances, step in to bring back the combined materials to a condition of separation by a process of dissociation carried into effect at the expense of that solar energy which is now supposed to be lost to our planetary system.

According to the law of dissociation as developed by Bunsen and Sainte-Claire Deville, the point of dissociation of different compounds depends upon the temperature on the one hand, and upon the pressure on the other. According to Sainte-Claire Deville, the dissociation tension of aqueous vapour of atmospheric pressure and at 2800° C. is 0·5, that is to say only half of the vapour can exist as such, its remaining half being found as a mechanical mixture of hydrogen and oxygen; but with pressure, the temperature of dissociation rises in the same ratio as the temperature of saturated steam rises with its pressure. It is therefore conceivable that the temperature of the solar photosphere may be raised by combustion to a temperature exceeding 2800° C.,[1] whereas dissociation may be effected in space at comparatively low temperatures.

These investigations had reference only to heats measured by means of pyrometers, but do not extend to the effects of radiant heat. Dr. Tyndall has shown by his elaborate researches that vapour of water and other gaseous compounds intercept radiant heat in a most remarkable degree, and there is other evidence to show that radiant energy from a source of high intensity possesses a dissociating power far surpassing the measurable temperature to which the compound substance under its influence is raised. Thus carbonic anhydride and water are dissociated in the leaf cells of plants, under the influence of the direct solar ray at ordinary summer temperature, and experiments in which I have been engaged for nearly three years[2] go to prove that this dissociating action is obtained also under the radiant influence of the electric arc, although it is scarcely perceptible if the source

[1] See pp. 58, 59 for other reasons why the temperature of the photosphere does probably not exceed 2800° C.

[2] See *Proc. Roy. Soc.*, vol. 30, p. 208, and paper read before Section A, British Association, and printed in full in the Report for 1881, Part I., p. 474.

of radiant energy is such as can be produced by the combustion of oil or gas.

The point of dissociation of aqueous vapour and carbonic anhydride admits, however, of being determined by direct experiment. It engaged my attention some years ago, but I have hesitated to publish the qualitative results I then obtained, in the hope of attaining to quantitative proofs.

These experiments consisted in the employment of glass tubes, furnished with platinum electrodes, and filled with aqueous vapour or with carbonic anhydride in the usual manner, the latter being furnished with caustic soda to regulate the vapour pressure by heating. Upon immersing one end of the tube charged with aqueous vapour in a refrigerating mixture of ice and chloride of calcium, its temperature at that end was reduced to $-32°$ C., corresponding to a vapour pressure, according to Regnault, of $\frac{1}{1800}$ of an atmosphere. When so cooled no slow electric discharge took place on connecting the two electrodes with a small induction coil. I then exposed the end of the tube projecting out of the freezing mixture, backed by white paper, to solar radiation (on a clear summer's day) for several hours, when upon again connecting up to the inductorium, a discharge, apparently that of a hydrogen vacuum, was obtained. This experiment being repeated furnished unmistakable evidence, I thought, that aqueous vapour had been dissociated by exposure to solar radiation. The carbonic anhydride tubes gave, however, less reliable results. Not satisfied with these qualitative results, I made arrangements to collect the permanent gases so produced by means of a Sprengel pump, but was prevented by lack of time from pursuing the inquiry, which I purpose, however, to resume shortly, being of opinion that, independently of my present speculation, the experiments may prove useful in extending our knowledge regarding the laws of dissociation.[1]

[1] Further experiments in this direction are still in progress, in which powerful arc light is substituted for solar rays. They furnish corroborative evidence, and will be made the subject-matter of a separate communication.

It should here be observed that, according to Professor Stokes, the ultra-violet rays are in a large measure absorbed in passing through clear glass, and it follows from this discovery that only a small portion of the chemical rays found their way through the tubes to accomplish the work of dissociation.

This circumstance being adverse to the experiment only serves to increase the value of the effect observed, whilst it appears to furnish additional proof of the fact, first enunciated by Professor Draper, and corroborated by my own experiments on plants, that the dissociating power of light is not confined to the ultra-violet rays, but depends as regards the process of vegetation chiefly upon the yellow ray.

Assuming, for my present purpose, that dissociation of aqueous vapour was really effected in the experiment just described, and assuming, further, that stellar space is filled with aqueous and other vapour of a density not exceeding the $\frac{1}{2000}$th part of our atmosphere, it seems reasonable to suppose that its dissociation would be effected by solar radiation, and that solar energy would thus be utilised.[1] The presence of carbonic anhydride and carbonic oxide would only serve to facilitate the decomposition of the aqueous vapour by furnishing substances to combine with nascent oxygen and hydrogen. It is not necessary to suppose that all the energy radiated from the Sun into space would be intercepted, inasmuch as even a partial return of heat in the manner described would serve to supplement solar radiation, the balance being lost to the Solar System. To this loss of energy must be added that involved in keeping up the circulating movement of the gases, which, however, would probably not be relatively greater than that concerned in the tidal retardation of the

[1] Mr. Faye has understood this passage to mean that I supposed stellar space to be filled with gases of this density, whereas it was the limit imposed by my experiment, and I have spoken of the gases in space as being *extremely attenuated*, which, according to Mr. Crookes, would mean about $\frac{1}{2000000}$ atmospheric pressure.

earth's rotation. By means of the fan-like action resulting from the rotation of the Sun, the vapours dissociated in space would be drawn towards the polar surfaces of the Sun, be heated by increase in density, and would burst into flame at a point where both their density and temperature had reached the necessary elevation to induce combustion, each complete cycle taking years or centuries to be accomplished. The resulting aqueous vapour, carbonic anhydride and carbonic oxide, would be drawn towards the equatorial regions, and be then again projected into space by centrifugal force.

Doubts have been expressed as to the sufficiency of the proof that dissociation of attenuated aqueous vapour and carbonic acid is really effected by radiant solar energy, and, if so effected, whether the amount of heat so supplied to the Sun could be at all adequate in amount to keep up the known rate of radiation. It was admitted in my paper that my own experiments on the dissociation of vapours within vacuum tubes amounted to inferential rather than absolute proof; but the amount of inferential evidence in favour of my views has been very much strengthened since by chemical evidence received from various sources; I will here only refer to one of these.

Professor Piazzi Smyth, the Astronomer Royal for Scotland, has, in connection with Professor Herschel of Newcastle, recently presented an elaborate paper or series of papers to the Royal Society of Edinburgh "On the Gaseous Spectra in Vacuum Tubes," of which he has kindly forwarded me a copy. It appears from these memoirs that when vacuum tubes, which contain attenuated vapours, have been laid aside for a length of time, they turn practically into hydrogen tubes. In another very recent paper presented to the Royal Society of Edinburgh, Professor Piazzi Smyth furnishes important additional proof of the presence of oxygen in the outer solar atmosphere, and gives an explanation why this important element has escaped observation by the spectroscope. Additional proof of the existence of oxygen in the outer solar atmosphere, has been given by Professor Stoney, the Astronomer Royal for Ireland, and by Mr. R. Meldola in an interesting paper communicated by him to the *Philosophical Magazine* in June, 1878.

As regards the sufficiency of an inflowing stream of dissociated vapours to maintain solar energy, the following calculation may be of service. Let it be assumed that the stream flowing in upon the polar surfaces of the Sun flashes into flame when it has attained the density of our atmosphere, that its velocity at that time is 100 feet per second (the velocity of a strong terrestrial wind) and that in its composition only one-twentieth part is hydrogen and marsh gas in equal proportions, the other nineteen-twentieths being made up of oxygen, nitrogen, and neutral compounds. It is well known that each pound of hydrogen develops in burning about 60,000 heat units, and each pound of marsh gas about 24,000; the average of the two gases mixed in equal proportion would yield, roughly speaking, 42,000 units; but, considering that only one-twentieth part of the inflowing current is assumed to consist of such combustible matter, the amount of heat developed per pound of inflowing current would be only 2,100 heat units. One hundred cubic feet, weighing eight pounds, would enter into combustion every second upon each square foot of the polar surface, and would yield $8 \times 60 \times 60 \times 2100 = 60{,}480{,}000$ heat units per hour. Assuming that one-third of the entire solar surface may be regarded as polar heat-receiving surface, this would give 20,000,000 heat units per square foot of solar surface; whereas according to Herschel's and Pouillet's measurements only 18,000,000 heat units per square foot of solar surface are radiated away. There would thus be no difficulty in accounting for the mainten-

CORONA AS OBSERVED BY PROFESSOR LANGLEY IN JULY, 1878

ance of solar energy from the supposed source of supply. On the other hand I wish to guard myself against the assumption that appears to have been made by some critics, that what I have advocated would amount to the counterpart of "perpetual motion," and therefore to an absurdity. The Sun cannot of course get back any heat radiated by himself which has been turned to a purpose; thus the solar heat spent upon our earth in effecting vegetation must be absolutely lost to him; but on the other hand the laws regarding the conservation of energy make it impossible to suppose that heat radiation into space can go on indefinitely without producing tangible effects regarding which we are up to the present without information.

My paper presented to the Royal Society was accompanied by a diagram of an ideal corona representing an accumulation of igneous matter upon the solar surfaces, surrounded by disturbed regions pierced by occasional cyclones and outbursts of metallic vapours, and culminating in two outward streams projecting from the equatorial surfaces into space through many thousands of miles. It was therefore a matter of great satisfaction to me to be informed, as I have been by an excellent authority and eye-witness, that my imaginary diagram bore a very close resemblance to the corona observed in America on the occasion of the total eclipse of the Sun on the 11th of January, 1880; a representation of this phenomenon as observed on the occasion of the previous eclipse—that of 1878—has appeared since in the official American Report, of which the diagram facing this page, taken by Professor Langley, is a copy.

Space would, according to my views, be filled with gaseous compounds in process of decomposition by solar radiant energy, and the existence of these gases seems to furnish an explanation of the solar absorption spectrum, in which the lines of some of the substances may be entirely neutralised and lost to observation. As regards the heavy metallic vapours revealed in the Sun by the spectroscope, it is assumed that these form a lower and denser solar atmosphere, not participating in the fan-like action which is supposed to affect the light outer atmosphere only, in which hydrogen is the principal factor.

Such a dense metallic atmosphere could not participate in the fan action affecting the lighter photosphere, because this is only feasible on the supposition that the density of the inflowing current is, at equal distances from the gravitating centre, equal or nearly equal to the outflowing current. It is true that the products of combustion of hydrogen and carbonic oxide are denser than their constituents, but this difference may be balanced by their superior temperature on leaving the Sun, whereas the metallic vapours would be unbalanced, and would therefore obey the laws of gravitation, recalling them to the Sun. On the surface of contact between the two solar atmospheres intermixture, induced by friction, must take place however, giving rise perhaps to those cyclones and explosive effects which are revealed to us by the telescope in the intermediate or stormy region of the Sun, and which have been commented on by Sir John Herschel and other astronomers. Some of the denser vapours would probably get intermixed and carried away mechanically by the lighter gases, and give rise to that cosmic dust which is observed to fall upon our earth in not inappreciable quantities. Excessive intermixture would be prevented by the intermediary neutral atmosphere, the penumbra.

As the whole Solar System moves through space at a velocity estimated at 150,000,000 of miles annually (being about one-fourth of the velocity of the earth in its orbit), it appears possible that the condition of the gaseous fuel supplying the Sun may vary according to its state of previous decomposition, in which action other heavenly bodies may have taken part. May it not be upon such differences in the quality of the fuel supplied that the observed variations of the solar heat may depend? and may it not be in consequence of such changes in the thermal condition of the photosphere that Sun-spots are formed?

The views here advocated could not be thought acceptable unless they furnished at any rate a consistent explanation of the still somewhat mysterious phenomena of the zodiacal light and of comets. Regarding the former, we should be able to return to Mairan's views, the objection by Laplace being met by a continuous outward flow from the solar equator. Luminosity would be attributable to particles of dust emitting light reflected from the Sun, or by phosphorescence. But there is another cause for luminosity of these particles which may deserve a passing consideration. Each particle would be electrified by gaseous friction in its acceleration, and its electric tension would be vastly increased in its forcible removal, in the same way as the fine dust of the desert has been observed by Werner Siemens to be in a state of high electrification on the apex of the Cheops Pyramid. Would not the zodiacal light also find explanation by slow electric discharge backward from the dust towards the Sun? and would the same cause not account for a great difference of potential between the Sun and earth, which latter may be supposed to be washed by the solar radial current? May not the presence of the current also furnish us with an explanation of the fact that hydrogen, while abounding apparently in space, is practically absent in our atmosphere, where aqueous vapour, which may be partly derived from the Sun, takes its place? An action analogous to this, though on a much smaller scale, may be set up also by terrestrial rotation, giving rise to an electrical discharge from the outgoing equatorial stream to the polar regions, where the atmosphere to be pierced by the return flood is of least resistance.

The effect of this continuous outpour of solar materials could not be without very important influences as regards the geological conditions of our earth. Geologists have long acknowledged the difficulty of accounting for the amount of carbonic acid that must have been in our atmosphere, at one time or another, in order to form with lime those enormous beds of dolomite and limestone, of which the crust of our earth is in great measure composed. It has been calculated that if this carbonic acid had been at one and the same time in our atmosphere it would have caused an elastic pressure fifty times that of our present atmosphere; and if we add the carbonic acid that must have been absorbed in vegetation in order to form our coal-beds, we should probably have to double that pressure. Animal life, of which we find abundant traces in these "measures," could not have existed under such conditions, and we are almost forced to the conclusion that the carbonic acid must have been derived from an external source.

It appears to me that the theory here advocated furnishes a feasible solution of this geological difficulty. Our earth being situated in the outflowing current of the solar products of combustion, or, as it were, in the solar chimney, would be fed from day to day with its quota of carbonic acid, of which our local atmosphere would assimilate as much as would be necessary to maintain in it a carbonic acid vapour density balancing that of the solar current; we should thus receive our daily supply of this important constituent (with the regularity of fresh rolls for breakfast), which, according to an investigation by M. Reiset, communicated to the French Academy of Sciences by M. Dumas on the 6th of March last, amounts to the constant factor of the three ten-thousandth part of our atmosphere. The aqueous vapour in the air would be similarly maintained as to its density, and its influx to, or reflux from, our atmosphere would be determined by the surface temperature of our earth.

It is also important to show how the phenomena of comets could be harmonised with the views here advocated, and I venture to hope that these occasional visitors will serve to furnish us with positive evidence in my favour. Astronomical physicists tell us that the nucleus of a comet consists of an aggregation of stones similar to meteoric stones. Adopting this view, and assuming that the stones have absorbed in stellar space gases to the amount of six times their volume, taken at atmospheric pressure, what, it may be asked, will be the effect of such a mass of stone advancing towards the Sun at a velocity reaching in perihelion the prodigious rate of 366 miles per second (as observed in the comet of 1845), being twenty-three times our orbital rate of motion. It appears evident that the entry of such a divided mass into a comparatively dense atmosphere must be accompanied by a rise of temperature by frictional resistance, aided by attractive condensation. At a certain point the increase of temperature must cause ignition, and the heat thus produced must drive out the occluded gases, which in an atmosphere say 3,000 times less dense than that of our earth would produce $6 \times 3{,}000 = 18{,}000$ times the volume of the stones themselves. These gases would issue forth in all directions, but would remain unobserved except in that of motion, in which they would meet the interplanetary atmosphere with the compound velocity, and form a zone of intense combustion, such as Dr. Huggins has lately observed to surround the one side of the nucleus, evidently the side of forward motion. The nucleus would thus emit original light, whereas the tail may be supposed to consist of stellar dust rendered luminous by reflex action produced by the light of the Sun and comet combined, as foreshadowed already by Tyndall and by Tait, starting each from different assumptions.

These are in brief the outlines of my reflections regarding this most fascinating question, which I now venture to put before the Royal Society. I have long had a conviction, derived principally from familiarity with some of the terrestrial effects of heat, that the prodigious and seemingly wanton dissipation of solar heat is unnecessary to satisfy accepted principles regarding the conservation of energy, but that this heat apparently expended without producing any effect whatever may be effectively arrested and returned over and over again to the Sun, in a manner somewhat analogous to the action of the heat recuperator in the regenerative gas furnace. The fundamental conditions are :—

1. That aqueous vapour and carbon compounds are present in stellar or interplanetary space.

2. That these gaseous compounds while in a state of extreme attenuation are capable of being dissociated by radiant solar energy.

3. That these dissociated vapours are capable of being compressed into the solar photosphere by a process of interchange with an equal amount of reassociated vapours, this interchange being effected by the centrifugal action of the Sun himself.

If these conditions could be substantiated, we should gain the satisfaction that our Solar System would no longer impress us with the idea of prodigious waste through dissipation of energy into space, but rather with that of well-ordered, self-sustaining action, capable of continuing solar radiation to a very remote future.

On Electrical Discharges in Vacuum Tubes and their Relation to Solar Physics.

An Extract from the Author's Presidential Address to the Meeting of the British Association at Southampton, August, 1882.

The means usually employed to produce electrical discharge in vacuum tubes was Ruhmkorff's coil; but Mr. Gassiot first succeeded in obtaining the phenomena by means of a galvanic battery of 3,000 Leclanché cells. Dr. De La Rue, in conjunction with his friend Dr. Hugo Müller, has gone far beyond his predecessors in the production of batteries of high potential. At his lecture "On the Phenomena of Electric Discharge," delivered at the Royal Institution in January, 1881, he employed a battery of his own invention consisting of 14,400 cells (14,832 Volts), which gave a current of 0·054 Ampère, and produced a discharge at a distance of 0·71 inch between the terminals. During last year he increased the number of cells to 15,000 (15,450 Volts), and increased the current to 0·4 Ampère, or eight times that of the battery he used at the Royal Institution.

With the enormous potential and perfectly steady current at his disposal, Dr. De La Rue has been able to contribute many interesting facts to the science of electricity. He has shown, for example, that the beautiful phenomena of the stratified discharge in exhausted tubes are but a modification and a magnification of those of the electric arc at ordinary atmospheric pressure. Photography was used in his experiments to record the appearance of the discharge, so as to give a degree of precision otherwise unattainable in the comparison of the phenomena. He has shown that between two points the length of the spark, provided the insulation of the battery is efficacious, is as the square of the number of cells employed. Dr. De La Rue's experiments have proved that at all pressures the discharge in gases is not a current in the ordinary acceptation of the term, but is of the nature of a disruptive discharge. Even in an apparently perfectly steady discharge in a vacuum tube, when the strata as seen in a rapidly revolving mirror are immovable, he has shown that the discharge is a pulsating one; but, of course, the period must be of a very high order.

At the Royal Institution, on the occasion of his lecture, he produced, in a very large vacuum tube, an imitation of the Aurora Borealis; and he has deduced from his experiments that the greatest brilliancy of Aurora displays must be at an altitude of from thirty-seven to thirty-eight miles—a conclusion of the highest interest, and in opposition to the extravagant estimate of 281 miles, at which it had been previously put.

The President of the Royal Society has made the phenomena of electrical discharge his study for several years, and resorted in his important experiments to a special source of electric power. In a note addressed to me, Mr. Spottiswoode describes the nature of his investigations much more clearly than I could venture to give them. He says: "It had long been my opinion that the dissymmetry, shown in electrical discharges through rarefied gases, must be an essential element of every disruptive discharge, and that the phenomena of stratification might be regarded as magnified images of features always present, but concealed under ordinary circumstances. It was with a view to the study of this question that the researches by Moulton and myself were undertaken. The method chiefly used consisted in introducing into the circuit intermittence of a particular kind, whereby one luminous discharge was rendered sensitive to the approach of a conductor outside the tube. The application of this method enabled us to produce artificially a variety of phenomena, including that of stratification. We were thus led to a series of conclusions relating to the mechanism of the discharge, among which the following may be mentioned:—

"1. That a stria, with its attendant dark space, forms a physical unit of a striated discharge; that a striated column is an aggregate of such units formed by means of a step-by-step process; and that the negative glow is merely a localised stria, modified by local circumstances.

"2. That the origin of the luminous column is to be sought for at its negative end; that the luminosity is an expression of a demand for negative electricity; and that the dark spaces are those regions where the negative terminal, whether metallic or gaseous, is capable of exerting sufficient influence to prevent such demand.

"3. That the time occupied by electricity of either name in traversing a tube is greater than that occupied in traversing an equal length of wire, but less than that occupied by molecular streams (Crooke's radiations) in traversing the tubes. Also that, especially in high vacua, the discharge from the negative terminal exhibits a durational character not found at the positive.

"4. That the brilliancy of the light with so little heat

may be due in part to brevity in the duration of the discharge; and that for action so rapid as that of individual discharges, the mobility of the medium may count as nothing; and that for these infinitesimal periods of time gas may itself be as rigid and as brittle as glass.

"5. That striæ are not merely loci in which electrical is converted into luminous energy, but are actual aggregations of matter.

"This last conclusion was based mainly upon experiments made with an induction coil excited in a new way—viz. directly by an alternating machine, without the intervention of a commutator or condenser. This mode of excitement promises to be one of great importance in spectroscopic work, as well as in the study of the discharge in a magnetic field, partly on account of the simplification which it permits in the construction of induction coils, but mainly on account of the very great increase of strength in the secondary currents to which it gives rise."

These investigations assume additional importance when we view them in connection with solar—I may even say stellar—physics, for evidence is augmenting in favour of the view that interstellar space is not empty, but is filled with highly attenuated matter of such a nature as may be put into our vacuum tubes. Nor can the matter occupying stellar space be said any longer to be beyond our reach for chemical and physical test. The spectroscope has already thrown a flood of light upon the chemical constitution and physical condition of the Sun, the stars, the comets, and the far distant nebulæ, which latter have yielded spectroscopic photographs under the skilful management of Dr. Huggins and Dr. Draper of New York. Armed with greatly improved apparatus, the physical astronomer has been able to reap a rich harvest of scientific information during the short periods of the last two solar eclipses: that of 1880, visible in America, and that of May last, observed in Egypt by Lockyer, Schuster, and by Continental observers of high standing. The result of this last eclipse expedition has been summed up as follows: "Different temperature levels have been discovered in the solar atmosphere; the constitution of the corona has now the possibility of being determined, and it is proved to shine with its own light. A suspicion has been aroused once more as to the existence of a lunar atmosphere, and the position of an important line has been discovered. Hydro-carbons do not exist close to the Sun, but may in space between us and it."

To me personally these reported results possess peculiar interest, for in March last I ventured to bring before the Royal Society a speculation regarding the conservation of solar energy, which was based upon the three following postulates, viz.:—

1. That aqueous vapour and carbon compounds are present in stellar or interplanetary space.

2. That these gaseous compounds while in a state of extreme attenuation are capable of being dissociated by radiant solar energy.

3. That the effect of solar rotation is to draw in dissociated vapours upon the polar surfaces, and to eject them after combustion back into space equatorially.

It is therefore a matter of peculiar gratification to me that the results of observations here recorded give considerable support to that speculation. The luminous equatorial extentions of the Sun which the American observations revealed in such a striking manner (with which I was not acquainted when writing my paper) were not observed in Egypt; but the outflowing equatorial streams which I suppose to exist could only be rendered visible by reflected sunlight, or by electric discharge between the particles of dust, which may be produced by solar disturbances. Professor Langley, of Pittsburg, has shown, by means of his bolometer, that the solar actinic rays are absorbed chiefly in the solar instead of in the terrestrial atmosphere, and Captain Abney has found, by his new photometric method, that absorption, due to hydro-carbons, takes place somewhere between the solar and terrestrial atmosphere; in order to test this interesting result still further, he has lately taken his apparatus to the top of the Riffel with a view of diminishing the amount of terrestrial atmospheric air between it and the Sun, and intends to bring a paper on this subject before Section A.[1] Stellar space filled with such matter as hydro-carbon and aqueous vapour would establish a material continuity between the Sun and his planets, and between the innumerable solar systems of which the universe is composed. If chemical action and reaction can further be admitted, we may be able to trace certain conditions of thermal dependence and maintenance, in which we may recognise principles of high perfection, applicable also to comparatively humble purposes of human life.

Letters on the Conservation of Solar Energy addressed to the Editor of "Nature."

On the Conservation of Solar Energy.

With your permission I should like to offer a few remarks upon the interesting paper of Dr. C. William Siemens on the "Conservation of Solar Energy," published in *Nature* (vol. xxv. p. 440). The main hypothesis upon which that paper is based, that of a fan-like action of the Sun, is not improbable; nor are the consequences drawn illogical, if we could reasonably imagine space to be occupied by such condensed molecules as he supposes. That space is everywhere occupied by matter there is no just reason to doubt. The hypothesis of an ether, specifically distinct from matter, is a gratuitous assumption, and one of the last surviving relics of eighteenth century science. Unless it can be proved that highly disintegrated matter is positively incapable of conveying light vibrations, there is no warrant for assigning this duty to a distinct form of substance. But that matter exists in outer space in the same conditions as in the planetary atmospheres is certainly improbable. Its duty as a

[1] See Appendix, p. 98.

conveyer of radiant vibrations seems to require a far greater tensity, and its disintegration is probably extreme.

If we assume, then, that matter exists throughout the universe, here as condensed spheres, there as highly rarefied substance, with the atmospheric envelopes of the spheres gradually shading off into the excessively rare matter of mid space; another hypothesis may be deduced, somewhat different to that offered by Dr. Siemens. The views which I desire to present have been already published, but they seem worthy of repetition in connection with his solar theory.

On the nebular hypothesis, the matter of the Sun was once disseminated through space. Gravitative attraction has, therefore, had a double effect. The greater portion of this matter is now drawn together into a contracted mass. The remaining portion yet occupies outer space, in a far more rarefied condition than the original. But an important consequence attends the condensation and rarefaction of gases. This is, that condensed gases become heated, rarefied gases cooled, and this without the aid of heat exchange with outer material. In the one case a portion of the absolute heat of the gas, formerly latent, becomes sensible; in the other a portion of the sensible heat becomes latent. If originally the absolute contents and the temperatures were alike equal, condensation and rarefaction would not, of themselves, change the heat contents, but they would change the temperatures. In condensation, the latent heat is reduced, the sensible heat increased, and the temperature rises. In rarefaction the opposite effect is produced, and the temperature falls.

This consideration applies as well to the problem of the condensation of nebulous as of terrestrial gases. The effect of contraction of nebulous gas into a dense sphere, must be a considerable rise in temperature if there be no diminution of absolute heat contents. The effect of rarefaction of the remaining matter of space must be a decrease in temperature. Thus, if radiant outflow of heat from the Sun had been prevented during his condensation, the eventual result must have been that the Sun and the matter of outer space would have continued equal, mass for mass, in absolute heat contents, and yet have become immensely different in temperature.

And from this must have come another interesting result, namely, that their degree of disintegration would continue the same. There could be no more chemical combination in the Sun, if thus retaining all his heat, than in the rare matter of space. For chemical condensation to take place, the heat contents must be reduced. An equal degree of absolute heat signifies an equal motive vigour of particles, and it is this motive vigour which enables them to resist chemical attraction. It may be supposed, however, that in dense matter the chemical attraction would be more effective from its increased energy through contiguity. Yet this is an erroneous idea; there is no real greater contiguity between the particles of dense than of rare matter. In both cases, the particles are brought incessantly into absolute contact through their vibrations. The number of contacts of dense as compared with rare matter may be millions to one, but that can have no effect upon the result. If the chemical vigour be stronger than the vibratory vigour, it will overcome it in the contact; if it be weaker, it will fail to overcome it, and a more frequent repetition of contacts cannot materially aid this result.

Thus all substances of equal absolute heat must be equal in degree of chemical integration, whatever their degrees of tensity or condensation. But the assumed equality of absolute heat cannot continue between dense and rare gases. The sensible heat of the dense gas tends to radiate out into the chilled rare gas. A constant and vigorous effort to equalise temperatures takes place. With every outflow of radiant heat from a sphere into space the absolute heat of the particles of the sphere decreases, that of the rare matter of space increases. The absolute heat contents grow more unequal with every step towards equalisation of temperatures. Consequently a variation in chemical condition arises. The loss of heat by the Sun, for instance, reduces the vibratory resistance to attraction, and with every such loss chemical molecules of greater complexity are formed. This heat is radiated into space. Probably some portion of this radiant heat is arrested and becomes local heat in the matter of space. If so the heat vigour of this matter increases, disintegration must ensue, and the increasing chemical condensation in the Sun must be matched by an increasing chemical disintegration in outer matter.

During the myriad years of solar condensation, this process of heat-outflow has been continuous, so that now, despite its great excess of temperature, the absolute heat of solar matter must be far below that of an equal mass of the matter of outer space. Can the heat thus lost by the Sun be recovered? If it could, the solar heat emissions might continue indefinitely. Dr. Siemens' hypothesis offers a method of recovery. If the matter of outer space is drawn into the solar atmosphere by such a polar inflow as he supposes, and subjected to the vigorous condensing influence of solar gravity, its volume must be very greatly decreased, and much of its latent heat become sensible. And as its absolute heat-contents are far in excess of those of solar matter, the result of such condensation must be a high degree of temperature, and a continual replacement of the radiated heat of the Sun. Without any chemical integration taking place in this inflowing matter, the solar temperature may be kept up by its mere condensation, and by rendering available its great excess of absolute heat. With chemical integration, and the consequent much greater condensation, of course the heat-yielding effect must be much more considerable.

This inflow of outer matter to the Sun is, in Dr. Siemens' hypothesis, rendered possible by a continuous outflow of solar matter to outer space, thus carrying substance of low heat energy to be mingled with the rarefied exterior matter, whose high heat energy is thereby somewhat reduced. Such a process, however, has in it something of the flavour of perpetual motion. The Sun is giving and taking, and his receptions may be equal to his emissions. He would thus constitute a machine yielding power to, and regaining power—to be again yielded—from the same substance. Yet there is another element in the case, which relieves it of this suspicious perpetual motion flavour. If the Sun is constantly flinging off rare matter at a tangent from his upper atmosphere, there must be a reaction upon the rotatory energy of the solar sphere. He must be gradually losing his energy of rotation, with extreme slowness, of course, since the weight thrown off is very light, but in time the effect cannot but become a marked one, and perhaps this loss of solar energy may be the ultimate source of the new heat obtained by such a process. We may conceive of a like process taking place, to a less marked extent, in the large and rapidly rotating planets, such as Jupiter.

CHARLES MORRIS.

PHILADELPHIA, U.S.

Under this title Dr. C. W. Siemens, on March 2, presented to the Royal Society a paper, which is published in *Nature*, vol. xxv. p. 440. Therein, after noticing the hypotheses proposed by Meyer, Helmholtz, and Sir William Thomson, to explain the maintenance of solar heat, he endeavours to show how the energy, apparently lost by radiation from the Sun into space, may be gathered up and restored to the centre of our system. This he conceives to be effected through the intervention of attenuated matter diffused throughout space, which is the recipient of the radiated energy, and is continuously absorbed and again reflected by the centrifugal action of the Sun himself. The matter diffused through space he supposes to include oxygen and nitrogen, hydrogen, aqueous vapour, and carbon compounds, besides solid materials which are probably exhalations from the Sun, and constitute the so-called cosmic dust.[1]

[1] In a paper on the subject of an interstellar medium, read by me before the French Academy of Sciences (*Comptes Rendus*, September 23, 1878, page 453), I spoke of it as affording, in accordance with the ideas of Newton and of Grove, a means of material communication between celestial bodies and added: "Cette théorie d'une échange universelle me paraissait fournir une explication de l'origine des poussières cosmiques."

In support of this view of an interstellary nature Dr. Siemens cites Grove and Mattieu Williams, among others, but does not seem aware that its agency, in gathering up and restoring to the Sun his lost radiant energy, has been maintained by these writers. Sir William Grove, in his address as President of the British Association in 1866, attempted to find in this interstellar matter (whose nature and relations to our atmosphere he had already considered in 1843, in his celebrated essay on "The Correlation of Forces") a source of solar heat, inasmuch as the Sun "may condense gaseous matters as it travels in space, and so heat may be produced." This same view suggests the title of "The Fuel of the Sun," by Mattieu Williams, a book published in 1860, the argument of which, as briefly resumed by me in an essay on "The Chemical and Geological Relations of the Atmosphere," in the *American Journal of Science* for May, 1880, is as follows:—

"The solar heat, according to Williams, is maintained by the Sun's condensation of the attenuated matter everywhere encountered by that body in his motion through interstellar space. The irregular movements impressed upon the Sun by the varying attractions of the planets, stirring up and intermingling the different strata of the solar atmosphere, and producing the great perturbations therein, of which the telescope affords evidence, are, in his hypothesis, the efficient agents in the process. The diffused matter or ether, which is the recipient of the heat-radiations of the universe, is thereby drawn into the depths of the solar mass; repelling thence the previously condensed and thermally-exhausted ether, it becomes compressed and gives up its heat, to be, in turn, itself driven out in a rarefied and cooled state, and to absorb a fresh supply of heat, which he supposes to be, in this way, taken up by the ether, and again concentrated and redistributed by the suns of the universe."

The astronomer must judge between the different views of the mechanism of what may be called the process of solar respiration in this hypothesis, as put forward by Siemens and

Williams respectively. We may call attention in this connection to Newton's *Principia*, book iii., proposition 12.

The views of Grove and of Williams, cited in my paper of 1880, are further considered in an essay on "Celestial Chemistry from the time of Newton," read by me in November, 1881, before the Philosophical Society of Cambridge, and reprinted from its *Proceedings* both in the *Chemical News* and the *American Journal of Science* for February, 1882. A perusal of this paper, to which Dr. Siemens alludes, will show that Sir Isaac Newton 200 years ago conceived the existence of an interstellar ether made up in part from emanations and exhalations from the atmospheres of the earth, the planets, and the Sun, and from comets. He further conjectured this interstellary medium to contain "the material principle of life" and "the food of Sun and planets," furnishing "the solary fuel," and being copiously absorbed by the Sun "to conserve his shining." The relations of this interstellary matter to terrestrial life I have endeavoured to set forth in the paper just noticed. In connection with Sir William Thomson's calculation of the density of the luminiferous medium therein mentioned, the reader is referred to a recent examination of the subject by P. Glan, in the *Annalen der Physik und Chemie*, No. viii. 1879, in which he concludes that the lower limit of density would be more than 7,000 times greater than that calculated by Thomson.

Dr. Siemens has, in his paper, further suggested that solar radiation may effect the dissociation in interstellar space of the compounds of oxygen with carbon and with hydrogen, so that these elements may reach the Sun in an uncombined state, and there be burned. He would thus make the Sun not only a compressing-engine, but a furnace. While such a dissociation in outer space is not impossible, it is to be said that a preliminary decomposition, followed by reunion in the solar sphere, would in no way augment the ultimate calorific effect of compression there. The elements in the act of dissociation in space would absorb just as much radiant energy as would be set free by their subsequent combination, so that, whether the solar radiations are expended in heating or in dissociating the diffused matter, the final result in the Sun would be the same. It may be further remarked, that from what we know of solar chemistry, dissociation of aqueous vapour and of carbonic dioxide is more likely to take place in the Sun himself than in the cold regions of outer space.

While, therefore, his suggested addition to the hypothesis seems, if not untenable, unnecessary, we are grateful to Dr. Siemens for again bringing before us the grand conception which dawned upon the mind of Newton, but has found its fuller expression in our own day, and, as I have endeavoured to show in the papers already noticed, gives us the elements of a rational Physiology of the Universe.

T. STERRY HUNT.

MONTREAL, CANADA, *April* 3, 1882.

In the two preceding letters, by American men of science of well-known position, one of the three postulates upon which I grounded my solar plan is granted, that of space filled with attenuated matter; the second and all-important one of the equatorial outflowing current is not objected to; but the third, that of dissociation of attenuated matter in space by means of arrested solar energy, is called in question. Both my critics think dissociation in space unnecessary for the maintenance of solar energy, or as Dr. Sterry Hunt very clearly puts it: "Whether the solar radiations are expended in *heating* or in *dissociating* the diffused matter, the final result in the Sun would be the same."

I would be disposed to agree with this dictum if taken as an abstract proposition, but I do not think that my critics can have subjected their view to calculation, the keystone without which the arch of speculation cannot be considered as secure. We know by experimental evidence that stellar space, and the matter filling it, are intensely cold, as proved by the winter temperature of the polar regions; moreover water exposed even in the tropics to free radiation while insulated from the warm earth, freezes to a considerable thickness during a single night.

Let us suppose that the attenuated matter in space has a temperature of 100°[1] on the absolute scale (being 174° below the freezing-point of water), and that it is 100,000 times more rarefied than when it reaches by adiabatic compression the solar photosphere. The rise of temperature due to this compression must be according to Rankine's well-known formula—

$$\tau_2 = \tau_1 \left(\frac{p_2}{p_1}\right)^{\frac{\gamma - 1}{\gamma} = \cdot 29} = 2819^\circ \text{ absolute},$$

and this would make the solar photosphere 2545° on the centigrade scale. This temperature is scarcely adequate to produce the solar luminosity, which must require one equalling, though probably not far exceeding, that of a powerful electric arc; but although a higher maximum temperature could be reached by compression through a wider range, very little of the heat due to it could be spared for the purpose of radiation into space, because the gases so refrigerated would obey the law of solar gravitation to a greater extent than the heated in-coming gases, and would certainly not pass away into space, unless acted upon by a considerable extraneous force. The mere passage of the solar orb through space at a majestic pace which does not exceed one quarter of our orbital velocity, could not possibly produce such a result, and even the fan action advocated in my paper would fail to work in opposition to a large determining influence of density on solar gravitation.

These conditions are entirely changed if we assume, in addition to adiabatic compression and re-expansion, a further source of heat such as is produced in combustion. One

[1] In my original and somewhat hurried reply to Professor Sterry Hunt, I assumed an initial temperature of 160° absolute, and an adiabatic compression to only $\frac{1}{3000}$ of the original volume. These figures would imply an action within too narrow a limit of the solar atmosphere, and I have taken the liberty of substituting figures more harmonious with the argument advanced by me elsewhere.

pound of hydrogen develops in burning about 60,000 heat units, and one pound of marsh gas 24,000 heat units. In my article upon this subject, published in the April number of the *Nineteenth Century,* I showed that if only one-twentieth portion of the gases streaming in upon the polar surfaces at the rate of 100 feet a second were combustible gases, they could produce an amount of heat more than sufficient to account for the entire solar radiation as determined by Herschel and Pouillet.

There is no reason for supposing that the instreaming gases would penetrate beyond the solar photosphere; they would flash into combustion whenever their temperature (by adiabatic compression) had reached the limit of spontaneous ignition, and the light igneous clouds so produced would flow on above the denser metallic vapours which form part of the permanent body of the Sun, towards the equatorial regions, whence they would pass into space at a temperature still exceeding, to some extent, that of the inflowing gases, the heat radiated into space being made up by combustion of photospheric matter.

The fan action itself would be produced, no doubt, at the expense of solar rotation; but, in order to appreciate this retarding influence at its true value, it must be borne in mind that the flow of gases, when once established, has only to be changed in direction, the velocity acquired by the inflowing gases being simply transferred to the outflowing current so that the amount of rotative force required need only be sufficient to cover frictional retardation. The very interesting leading article in last week's *Nature,* regarding the solar observations in America during the last eclipses, now published for the first time, furnishes an unexpected and most striking corroboration of the solar fan action which I had ventured to put forward as a necessary consequence of solar rotation in space filled with attenuated matter.

I am well aware that my paper read before the Royal Society does scant justice to those who have devoted much time and ingenuity to the subject of solar physics, and that, moreover, many points of considerable interest connected with the views I advocate have been indicated only, instead of having been fully developed; but, on the whole, I thought it was better to present my views in mere outline before an audience well acquainted with our present information regarding solar physics, and with only half an hour's time at their disposal.

The elaboration of such a subject would necessitate the writing of a book rather than of a paper, and perhaps Dr. Sterry Hunt, who has already done so much to elucidate our present knowledge of solar physics, may be induced to extend his labours in this direction.

C. W. SIEMENS.

12, QUEEN ANNE'S GATE, WESTMINSTER,
April 26, 1882.

CONSERVATION OF SOLAR ENERGY.

WHILE Dr. Siemens's novel and ingenious theory described in his paper before the Royal Society, and published in *Nature*, will doubtless be adequately criticised in its more physical aspects by those who are better acquainted than myself with "the intricacies of solar physics," I may perhaps be allowed to point out one or two conclusions which appear somewhat opposed to the laws of mechanics. The author, for example, lays great stress upon the "high rotative velocity of the Sun," which at the solar equator, according to his figures, is four and a half times that at the terrestrial equator. To this "high rotative velocity" Dr. Siemens attributes the supposed expulsion from the solar equator of the products of combustion of the gases drawn in by the assumed fan action at the solar poles.

Mairan apparently thought the equatorial rise of the solar atmosphere due to the centrifugal force engendered by this velocity sufficient to account for the appearance of the zodiacal light, and according to Dr. Siemens his supposition may possibly be correct, if we suppose that space, instead of being an ether-vacuum, is filled with highly attenuated gases. It seems, however, that La Place, acting on the usual supposition of an empty stellar space, calculated that the solar atmosphere could not extend more than 9-20ths of the distance of Mercury, or about 16,000,000 miles, at which distance it would exist in such a highly rarefied condition as almost to merit the designation of vacuum. That this must be so, is evident when we remember that the high superficial velocity at the solar equator, though relatively larger than that at the terrestrial equator in the proportion given by Dr. Siemens, so far from being able to exert a powerful centrifugal force, is in this respect far less effective than the smaller tangential velocity at the terrestrial equator. This is chiefly due to the counteracting influence of solar gravity, which, as is well known, is more than twenty-seven times terrestrial gravity as represented by g. It is also partly due to the large value of the solar radius, since this also enters into the denominator of the expression for centrifugal force in terms of the tangential velocity, viz. $\frac{v^2}{r}$. It is at least remarkable that Dr. Siemens has made no allusion to either of these factors, which so intimately affect the centrifugal *efficiency* of the centrifugal force—the motive-power on which the entire action depends—and has made it appear from his language that this is a mere simple function of the tangential velocity at the solar equator.

As it is, owing to these united circumstances, but mainly to the former, the ratio of the centrifugal force acting on a particle to its weight is, even at the solar equator, almost infinitesimal.

To accentuate this astronomical platitude it is only necessary to quote figures which may be found in every popular work on the Sun, such as the fact that while the centrifugal force at the terrestrial equator deprives a body of 1-289th of its weight at the poles, the amount it would similarly lose at the solar equator would be 1-18,000th.

Or again, to put it in another light, in order that solar gravity and centrifugal force may equilibrate, and a particle at the solar equator be without weight, the Sun would have to turn upon his axis 133 times as fast as at present, while in order that the same conditions should prevail on the earth, its rotational velocity would only need to be increased seventeen times.

Except, therefore, where they would be momentarily affected by the local expulsive forces engendered by solar combustion, the different layers of the solar atmosphere would arrange themselves in the order of their relative densities, and remain quietly attached to the surface of the Sun, under an attraction fully twenty-seven times greater than that which our earth exerts on its aerial envelope. That, under such circumstances, the centrifugal force of the Sun could cause him to *project* into space the products of combustion seems most improbable.

Moreover, suppose, for the sake of argument, that this action really does take place, can it be literally maintained, according to Dr. Siemens's concluding sentence, that this action is "capable of perpetuating solar radiation to the *remotest* future"?[1] The laws of energy tell us that work cannot be done without expenditure of energy, and since the *primum mobile* in this case is solar rotation, and the gases entering at the solar poles must gradually acquire rotational momentum at the Sun's expense, they must, in time, reduce it to nought, when the supposed regenerative action would cease, and so the Sun burn out. In any case, therefore, the word "remotest" can only be understood to have a limited signification.

E. DOUGLAS ARCHIBALD.

[1] The expression used in the concluding paragraph of my original paper was certainly calculated to mislead, although in the body of the paper I speak of various losses of solar energy, showing that I did not contemplate *actio in perpetuum*.

[To save time we submitted Mr. Archibald's letter to Dr. Siemens, who sends the following reply.—Ed.]

This letter shows that Mr. Archibald has missed the principal point of my argument concerning solar fan action. I showed pretty clearly, I thought, that solar gravitation would affect the inflowing and the outflowing currents equally, and that centrifugal action must determine motion in the equatorial direction in a space filled with matter. But, to put the problem into a mathematical garb, let us consider the condition of two equal masses m_p and m_a, both at the radius R from the solar centre, the one opposite either pole, and the other opposite the equatorial region. The force of gravitation acting on these masses will be represented respectively by $\frac{gm_p}{R^2}$ and $\frac{gm_a}{R^2}$, and supposing both masses to be gaseous, and of the same chemical composition and temperature, they will represent equal volumes, say one cube foot.

These conditions being granted, we may put—

$$\frac{gm^p}{R^2} = \frac{gm_a}{R^2},$$

but the mass m_a is subject to another force, that produced by tangential motion, which shall be represented by v, and the centrifugal force resulting from this motion by ϕv; the force of gravitation towards the Sun will then be reduced to $\frac{gm_a}{R^2} - m_a\phi v$, and the latter factor being a positive quantity we have—

$$\frac{gm_p}{R^2} > \frac{gm_a}{R^2} - m_a\phi v.$$

This inequality of attractive forces must determine motion toward the Sun in favour of $\frac{gm_p}{R^2}$, and this condition holding good for any value of g and R, it follows that the polar inflow and equatorial outflow must take place, provided only that space is not empty, as supposed by La Place, but filled with either an elastic or non-elastic fluid.

To put it in another way, Mr. Archibald imagines that in order to determine an outflow from the Sun it is necessary for the centrifugal force $m_a\phi v$ to exceed the force of gravitation $\frac{gm_a}{R^2}$, whereas, according to my view, the value of the former determines only the rate of outflow, but is immaterial as regards the principle of action. The projection of dust is entirely dependent upon the outflowing current. I leave it for Mr. Archibald to determine for himself the velocity of current necessary to move a particle of dust of given size and weight away from the Sun in opposition to his force of gravity, which I am well aware is twenty-seven times that of the earth on its surface.

The gaseous current is of course produced at the expense of solar rotation, but this expenditure of energy is relatively much smaller than that lost to our earth through tidal action, and may be neglected for our present purposes. It is moreover counterbalanced by solar shrinkage as explained in my paper. C. WM. SIEMENS.

Dr. Siemens's Solar Hypothesis.

I have been waiting for several weeks for answers to the following rather obvious objections to Dr. Siemens's Solar Hypothesis, but I have not seen them either asked by others or answered by Dr. Siemens.

1. How the interplanetary gases near the Sun acquire a sufficient radial velocity to prevent their becoming a dense atmosphere round him?

2. Why enormous atmospheres have not long ago become attached to the planets, notably to the moon?

3. Why the earth has not long ago been deluged when a constant stream of aqueous vapour that would produce a rain of more than 30 inches per annum all over the earth must annually pass out past the earth in order to supply fuel to be dissociated by the heat that annually passes the earth?

4. Why we can see the stars although most of the solar radiations are absorbed within some reasonable distance of the Sun?

GEO. FRAS. FITZGERALD.

40, TRINITY COLLEGE, DUBLIN,
May 16, 1882.

I have the pleasure to reply to the very pertinent questions put by Prof. Fitzgerald as follows:—

1. The gases being for the most part hydrogen and hydrogen compounds, have a low specific gravity as compared with the denser gases forming the permanent solar atmosphere. On flashing into flame in the photosphere, their specific gravity would be vastly diminished, thus giving rise to a certain rebound action which, coupled with their acquired onward motion and with the centrifugal impulse they receive by frictional contact with the lower atmosphere, constitutes them a surface stream flowing from the polar to the equatorial regions, and thence out into space. (Lest I should be misunderstood, allow me to add that I do not look upon centrifugal action as sufficing in any way to overcome solar gravitation.) Astronomers are in the habit of regarding each spheroid possessed of an atmosphere as rotating in vacuous space; under such circumstances the atmosphere must partake of the rotatory motion of the solid spheroid, and after having attained an increased depth at the equator, will assume a state of static equilibrium unless disturbed by external influences. No such statical equilibrium is possible, however, if we assume the same spheroid with its atmosphere, surrounded by an ocean of indefinite dimensions, consisting of gaseous matter not partaking of the rotation of the spheroid, although subject to its attractive influence. Equal masses will under those conditions be equally attracted both in the polar and equatorial direction, and the continued disturbance of equilibrium by rotatory motion must result in continuous outflow. Nor need this outflow be accomplished entirely at the expense of rotatory motion of the spheroid because the inflowing polar current, when once established, will only have

to be changed in direction by frictional action in order to convert it into the outflowing current.

2. Regarding the second question, I assume that the atmosphere of each spheroid in space is precisely such as would result from its mass, and if this view is correct, the moon also must have an atmosphere, though of so attenuated a character as to be scarcely perceptible by means of optical instruments; for as Wollaston put it in his celebrated paper read before the Royal Society in January, 1822, "it would not be greater than that of our atmosphere is, where the earth attraction is equal to that of the moon at her surface, or about 5,000 miles from the earth's surface." I am well aware that in assuming atmospheric air to be a perfectly elastic fluid, the atmospheric density would, at a height of only 70 kilometers, not exceed the 1-7000th part of atmospheric density, and would therefore at greater distances become inappreciable; but we have evidence to show that Boyle and Mariotte's law holds good only within comparatively narrow limits,[1] and there is other evidence referred to in my paper in favour of the supposition that such gases as are contained in meteorites are diffused through space in appreciable amounts, or the meteorites could not for millions of years have retained these gases, notwithstanding the action of diffusion into empty space.

3. The amount of vapour that would condense upon the earth under the conditions here assumed, would depend upon its mean temperature on the one hand, and on the vapour-density of the stellar atmosphere surrounding it on the other. Assuming the density of the stellar atmosphere, which, while surrounding the earth does not partake of its rotatory motion, to be 1-10,000th part of atmospheric density, and saturated with aqueous vapour, the point of condensation would be, according to Regnault, $-50°$ C.;[2] if the outer regions of our atmosphere should be at that temperature, and saturated with

[1] See footnote under page 7.

[2] This assumed temperature is decidedly too high; if we assume it to be 100° absolute on the Centigrade scale, we should find a much lower vapour-density in space, but one which Regnault's formula does not give us the means of estimating.

aqueous vapour, the two would be in diffusive balance; if they were at a lower temperature they would acquire, and if at a higher they would part with, aqueous vapour to the surrounding medium.

4. It has long been held by astronomers that there are stars beyond our range of vision, which hypothesis would involve that of absorption of heat and light rays in stellar space; some rays are more easily absorbed than others; thus it appears to be the yellow ray which is most efficacious in the decomposition of carbonic acid and aqueous vapour in the vegetable cell. May not the same conditions prevail in space, and allow probably the rays of highest refrangibility to pass on to the greatest distance without being absorbed—I should say utilized—in doing chemical work?

C. WM. SIEMENS.

12, QUEEN ANNE'S GATE, S.W.,
May 22, 1882.

ON THE CONSERVATION OF SOLAR RADIATION.

IT appears to me a difficulty arises with regard to Dr. Siemens's theory when we consider the original condition of the earth and of the other planets. What, in fact, has become of the great amount of energy which was present in the form of heat in those bodies?

Just as in the case of the Sun, the rotation of the earth would produce a continuous cycle current, the decrease of rotatory energy being perhaps counterbalanced by shrinkage, the radiant heat would become transformed into the potential energy of dissociation, and this energy again would be given back to the earth in the form of heat in another part of the circuit where the elements recombine. Now it is quite impossible that the whole of the heat radiated should be used in this way, for after a lapse of years we should find a considerable diminution of potential, or (perhaps) rotatory energy, and we therefore should be forced to the conclusion that the earth became continually hotter. Hence some of the radiant heat escaped must have escaped into space, never to return.

Is it then a feasible solution that more heat is radiating from the Sun than is necessary for the dissociation of the elements? If so, then at least we should have a satisfactory explanation of its slowly-diminishing activity. G. B. S.

THE writer of this letter is right in concluding that in accordance with my hypothesis the earth also must throw out a stream of matter equatorially into space; and if your correspondent will refer to my article in the *Nineteenth Century* of April last, he will find that at p. 522 I speak of such a terrestrial outflow, with which I connect the phenomena of Aurora Borealis. If at any period of the world's history the rotatory velocity of the earth has been much greater than it is now (as has been suggested lately by Mr. G. Darwin), and its surface-temperature sufficiently high to cause ignition of combustible gases, it may be reasonably supposed that it had the power of recuperating its heat of radiation. The amount of heat so recuperated would, under all circumstances, be less than that received back by combustion, and the result of gradual diminution of temperature would be that on a certain day the temperature must have fallen below the point of ignition, from which day forward no further recuperation of heat can have taken place. The process of cooling would then proceed at a very rapid ratio, until the surface-temperature had reached another point of comparative constancy, at which the radiation into space was balanced by the heat received by solar radiation, which is our present condition.[1]

C. W. SIEMENS.

12, QUEEN ANNE'S GATE, S.W.,
October 16, 1882.

[1] Professor E. J. Stone lately called my attention to a most interesting observation favouring my solar hypothesis, viz., that when (probably by collision) a star, say of the third, suddenly lights up to one of the first magnitude, the greater brilliancy thus produced by its increased temperature rapidly subsides until its former degree of brilliancy is again reached, from which time forward its condition is maintained, apparently by a process of recuperation depending upon its rotation.

ON DR. C. W. SIEMENS'S NEW THEORY OF THE SUN. BY M. FAYE.

A Communication addressed to the Académie des Sciences, and published in the Comptes Rendus, *October 9th,* 1882.[1]

IT would appear that this theory has greatly struck our physicists; for it had scarcely appeared in London when it was translated and published in France in various forms, and especially in the last number of the *Annales de Chimie et de Physique.* I suppose that the principal object of this haste was the announcement of fresh experiments which have been instituted by the author upon the chemical action of light. It is well known that, under the action of light *and with the intervention of the chlorophyll of plants,* aqueous vapour and carbonic acid are decomposed at ordinary temperatures, and brought back to the combustible form, carbon and hydrogen variously associated. Dr. Siemens has tried whether the action of the light of the Sun alone would not produce this decomposition if we submit to him, without any other intermediary, aqueous vapour and carbonic-acid gas excessively rarefied, brought for example to the vacuum of $\frac{1}{1800}$. His experiments, which, in my opinion, only require a counter-test which it would be easy to institute, have given perfectly affirmative results. Thus, the burnt gases having been brought to such a rarefaction that they no longer permitted the passage of the induction-spark, a few hours' exposure to the light of the Sun sufficed to enable the mixture to allow this spark to pass with the well-known colouration that it acquires in hydro-carburetted media.[2]

Regarding these beautiful experiments as decisive, Dr. Siemens has been led to inquire whether this phenomenon does not perform in the universe a part still more consider-

[1] This communication was translated in the *Philosophical Magazine* of November, whence the present translation is taken.

[2] A vacuum produced in a bell-glass into which a drop of oil of turpentine has previously been introduced, for example.

able than in vegetable life. Supposing space to be filled with analogous gases, already burnt, the light of the Sun would revivify the combustibles hydrogen and carbon, which would then be quite ready to furnish the food of a fresh combustion.

By drawing them to himself and burning them afresh, the Sun would recuperate a good portion of the enormous heat which one is grieved to see him radiating in pure loss into celestial space.

Dr. Siemens has thus been lead to put forward the following hypothesis:—Space is filled with burnt gases, aqueous vapour and carbonic acid, mixed with inert gases, nitrogen, &c., pretty nearly the same as those of our atmosphere, at a pressure of $\frac{1}{2000}$. These gases are partially converted into combustibles under the action of solar light; then, by a mechanism like that of a fan of a blower, the Sun draws them to himself, burns them, and sends them back again into space. This immense source of heat would be continually resuscitated; the only part of its radiation lost would be that which is not absorbed by the cosmical medium of a density of $\frac{1}{2000}$.

It is perfectly true that, for the physicist, air at $\frac{1}{2000}$ would be an almost absolute vacuum, so much so indeed that in such a vacuum the electric spark would no longer pass. But to the astronomer such a medium would be very dense. When we speak, in Astronomy, of the resistance of a medium or of the ether, and when by the aid of the most delicate observations and the most profound calculations, we seek for traces of this resistance, we have to do with a very different thing.

Without entering upon these discussions, I will remark that the trajectory of a cannon-ball with a velocity of 500 metres is sufficiently altered at the end of a few seconds, to compel artillerists to take into account the resistance of the air in their tables.

If the air is reduced to $\frac{1}{2000}$, but the velocity of the projectile becomes that of the celestial movements, sixty times as much for example, these palpable effects will become, for a multitude of celestial projectiles of dimensions comparable to those of our cannon-balls, twice as great as in our firing-grounds, and this not merely at the end of a few years or a few centuries, but at the end of a few seconds.

In the second place, it seems to me that the celebrated English physicist has somewhat neglected to examine into the quantity of matter which he adds to the solar system. Under the influence of attraction this matter would go to unite itself with the pre-existing stars, with the Sun especially, and would continually augment their mass. Nothing is easier than to form an idea of this. A litre of air containing the required proportion of aqueous vapour weighs at least 1 gramme at the ordinary pressure. At a pressure of $\frac{1}{2000}$ this will be 0·0005 gramme, and a cubic metre will weigh 0·0005 kilogramme. This being settled, if we restrict the Solar System to a sphere including all the planets as far as Neptune, the weight of the excessively rarefied matter added by the hypothesis would be, in kilogrammes—

$$\tfrac{4}{3}\pi\,(6400000 \times 24000 \times 30)^3 \times 0{\cdot}0005 \text{ kilog.}$$ [1]

The actual weight of the Sun is, in kilogrammes—

$$\tfrac{4}{3}\pi\,(64000000)^3 \times 5{\cdot}6 \times 324000.$$ [2]

The first is 100,000 times as great as the second. It is therefore 100,000 times the mass of the Sun that this hypothesis adds to those of which celestial mechanics has hitherto kept so minute an account.

It is not very probable that the astronomers will adopt such hypotheses. No doubt they would be pleased to think that Nature has provided the Sun with resources to make his heat last longer; but as his final refrigeration is still, under any circumstances, a tolerably distant catastrophe, they will console

[1] The first number is the radius of the earth in metres; the second the distance of our globe from the Sun in terrestrial radii; the third the distance of Neptune in parts of the distance of the Sun.

[2] The first number is the radius of the earth in decimetres; the second the mean density of our globe referred to that of water; the third the mass of the Sun referred to that of the earth.

themselves by the thought that the things of this world, even the most beautiful, do not appear to be made to last for ever.

As to the fundamental experiments of Dr. Siemens, they will lose none of their importance in their eyes. The business is to surprise a secret of living nature, one of the laws of the organic world; and their desire will be that Dr. Siemens may pursue the course in which he has commenced so brilliantly, even though they cannot hope to have a very bright light thrown by it upon their own researches.

Reply to the Objections Presented by M. Faye against Mr. C. W. Siemens's New Theory of the Sun.

Letter of Mr. C. W. Siemens to M. Dumas, and published in the Comptes Rendus, *October 30th,* 1882.[1]

I HAVE studied the note published by M. Faye in the *Comptes Rendus* of October 9th, headed "On the New Theory of the Sun by Mr. C. W. Siemens." This communication has induced me to address to you some supplementary explanations, trusting that you will be so good as to communicate them to the Académie des Sciences, should you think them worthy of that honour.

When I communicated to the Royal Society of London on the 20th of February, 1882, my memoir "On the Conservation of Solar Energy," I did not expect or desire that the astronomical hypothesis, to which I had been led by observations in the domain of physics, would be accepted without objections. It was therefore with great pleasure that I saw in the *Annales de Chimie et de Physique* a translation of my memoir in the more extended and generalised form in which I had given it in the April number of the *Nineteenth Century*, and it was a source of still greater satisfaction to find that an astronomer of the high reputation of M. Faye had deemed it worthy of discussion before the Académie des Sciences.

[1] This letter was in part translated in the *Philosophical Magazine* of December, 1882.

M. Faye, while approving generally of the physical part of my investigations, questions their application to astronomy, and for the following reasons :—

1. That the presence of a universal gaseous medium at a pressure of $\frac{1}{2000}$ atmosphere would oppose an excessive resistance to the movements of the planets; 2. That this vapour, thus distributed, would be gradually attracted towards the Sun, and would tend to augment his mass considerably.

Allow me to point out, as regards the second of M. Faye's objections, that the degree of diffusion supposed by me to obtain in space is such as will ensure the permanence of the statical equilibrium between the forces of expansion and diffusion on the one hand, and of attraction towards the Sun and the celestial bodies on the other. If no such equilibrium were established, M. Faye's objection would at once upset my theory. I am, moreover, inclined to admit that if Mariotte's law with regard to the tension of gases was to hold good indefinitely, the pressure of the interplanetary gaseous medium would be reduced almost beyond anything of which we can form a conception; but it seems to me, from considerations drawn from the dynamical theory of gases, and from the manner in which, as demonstrated by Mr. Crookes, gases behave when rarefied to an extraordinary degree in tubes—it seems to me, I say, that there exists no *a priori* reason why this law should be extended rigorously to vapours beyond the confines of our atmosphere and of that of the Sun.[1]

As regards M. Faye's first objection, I admit that a density of $\frac{1}{2000}$ atmosphere would have the consequences which he so correctly establishes; and I remember having said, (see *Proceedings of the Royal Society*, p. 395,) that assuming the results of my experiments on the dissociation of vapours by solar energy to be proved, and assuming further that stellar space is filled with vapour at a pressure *not exceeding* the limit of $\frac{1}{2000}$ atmosphere, which corresponds to the highest rarefaction that I was able to obtain in my experiments, a dissociation of this cosmical vapour must ensue by means of

[1] See also footnote to p. 7.

the radiation of the Sun. It should be observed that this passage only relates to the physical phenomena submitted to my experiments, and that if the dissociation of aqueous vapour and of carbon-compounds is effected by the direct radiation of the Sun at so high a pressure as $\frac{1}{2000}$ atmosphere, it would, *a fortiori*, be effected in the more rarefied medium.

In another passage of my memoir, (p. 397,) when I apply my hypothesis to comets, I assume that, even at their perihelion, they move in a medium of a density not exceeding $\frac{1}{3000}$ atmosphere, and that this density would suffice to give rise to incandescence by frictional compression. This proves, at any rate indirectly, that I regarded stellar space as filled with vapour of a pressure much below $\frac{1}{3000}$ atmosphere, and (in the absence of all data of experiment and observation) I spoke of the stellar medium as in an *extremely rarefied* state, without fixing any limit to this rarefaction.

Since then new facts of observation have tended to confirm my hypothesis of a stellar space filled with rarefied matter analogous to that which we can actually produce in our vacuum-tubes. The equatorial prolongations of the solar atmosphere observed in America during the eclipse of 1880 seem to demonstrate the existence of matter extending from the Sun for several millions of leagues, and rendered visible, no doubt, by solid particles, illuminated partly by the reflection of the solar light, and partly by discharges of electricity from particle to particle towards the Sun.

My hypothesis has found a still more direct confirmation in the remarkable spectroscopic investigations communicated by Capt. Abney to Section A of the British Association in the month of August last, which prove that carbon-compounds of the ethyl or alcohol group exist, at a low temperature, between the Sun's atmosphere and our own, and recent observations made in America by Prof. Langley with his bolometer (although made with a totally different object in view) tend to confirm the results obtained by Capt. Abney upon the Riffel. We may also add to these proofs the interesting observation of Prof. Schwedöff (communicated to Section A of the British Association by Prof. Silvanus Thompson), according to which large hailstones, seemingly of cosmical origin, have on certain occasions been observed to fall upon the earth.

Accepting these observations as founded upon facts, physical considerations are not wanting for the approximate determination of stellar vapour density, which, in this case must be a function of the temperature in space. As Gorschow, on 30th November, 1871, observed a temperature of —63° C. in the Arctic regions, it follows that the stellar medium (which, if it consists of a vapour, is capable of intercepting calorific rays) must be at a temperature comprised between —63° and the absolute zero (—274°).

It is to Regnault that we owe our most exact knowledge of the density of vapours at different temperatures; but his researches did not extend below —32° C., and his formulæ cannot be rigorously applied below that point; nevertheless they enable us to estimate approximately what may be the densities of a vapour at lower temperatures; and it is thus that we are led to believe that at —130° the density of aqueous vapour does not exceed $\frac{1}{3000000}$ atmosphere. If we assume, further, that the gaseous mass which fills space consists only one-fifth of aqueous vapour, the other four-fifths being composed of hydrocarbons, carbonic acid, and nitrogen, the total pressure of the vapour cannot exceed $\frac{1}{1000000}$ atmosphere.

These vapours would traverse space with a velocity equal, probably, to half the tangential velocity at the surface of the Sun, or about 1 kilometre per second. It could be easily demonstrated that a column of these dissociated gases travelling with this velocity towards the polar surfaces of the Sun, and taken at a distance of 5,500,000 kilom. from the Sun (the mean distance of Mercury, the nearest of his planets) would present a sectional area of flow towards the Sun equal to 140,000 milliards of square kilometres, much more than sufficient to furnish the material necessary to yield by combustion the heat required to maintain the solar radiation.

Perhaps the eminent Director of the Bureau des Longitudes may be inclined to think that a gaseous medium of a density equal at most to $\frac{1}{1000000}$ of that of our atmosphere might still interfere with planetary movements to a degree incompatible with the facts ascertained by astronomical observations. If this be the case, it would suffice to assume a still lower temperature in space, and consequently a still more attenuated rarefaction of the interstellar gaseous matter.

On Mr. C. W. Siemens's New Theory of the Sun. By M. G. A. Hirn.

A communication addressed to the Académie des Sciences, and published in the Comptes Rendus, *November 6th,* 1882.[1]

To the grave objection brought forward by M. Faye against Mr. Siemens's new theory of the conservation of solar energy, another, also a very serious one, may be added. This objection may be summed up in few words.

Up to the present time there is no general agreement as to the real value of the Sun's temperature. Père Secchi carried it to millions of degrees. Other physicists, especially in France, lowered it to about twenty thousand degrees. According to the magnificent experiments of Mr. Langley (of Alleghany) this latter amount is, at any rate, a minimum. What is certain then, starting from the fine memoirs upon dissociation of our lamented colleague Henri Sainte-Claire Deville, is that none of the chemical compounds that we know upon our earth could exist at the surface of the Sun. All, even those which are most refractory in our laboratories, would be dissociated and reduced to their constituent elements. And this is what is admitted in M. Faye's theory of the Sun.

[1] This communication was translated in the *Philosophical Magazine* of December, whence the present translation is taken.

The natural and direct consequences of the preceding fact is, that the chemical compouuds which Mr. Siemens supposes to be dissociated by degrees in space by solar radiation, might certainly, in returning under the action of gravity and in the elementary state towards the central body, become reformed, and regenerate the heat expended in their dissociation in space; but this recombination could only be effected at an appreciable distance from the solar photosphere, and the compounds reproduced, on falling into the bosom of the latter, would be again completely dissociated. This action, therefore, would cause the expenditure of all the heat previously developed by the combination. From this it follows evidently that this return of the elements towards the centre would contribute nothing at all towards the conservation, or rather the continuous reproduction, of the solar temperature.

It seems to me that Mr. Siemens's theory may be subjected to another decisive critical test. If the solar radiation, or say the heat, whether visible or not, emitted or sent off by any celestial body during its course, effects the chemical dissociation of the hypothetical compounds disseminated in stellar space, the intensity of this radiation must necessarily be reduced by the positive work effected, and all that serves for this work is lost for the visibility of the star.

From this, then, it follows that the lustre of the Sun, of the stars, and of the planets must diminish according to a *much more rapid* law than that of the inverse proportion of the square of the distances. I say *much more* rapid; but we must say *extremely rapid.* In fact, from the moment when the recombination of the elements at the surface of the Sun would be capable of regenerating the heat emitted, it is evident that all this emitted heat would be employed in its turn in dissociating the chemical compounds in space. In order that the Sun could be thus continually maintained in its energy, it would be necessary that the distance at which it is visible, far from being unlimited as it probably is, should, on the contrary, be restricted; for wherever it would be still visible there would be light *not employed in chemical dissociation,* and consequently there would still be a definite loss *possible.* Nothing in the aspect of our planets and their satellites, it seems to me, authorises us to assume that there is any other reduction in the brilliancy of the light than that resulting from the inverse proportion of the square of their distance from the central body. We see stars the light of which has taken at least three years, and others of which the light has perhaps taken thousands of years to reach us. None of this light, therefore, has been employed in chemical dissociation; nothing could have been restored to them by the mode indicated by the ingenious theory of Mr. Siemens.

May I be permitted, in concluding this note, to revert to the objection formulated by M. Faye, and to render it in some degree palpable by a numerical example? In an extensive work upon which I am engaged, upon the constitution of stellar space, I naturally examine into the consequences that the resistance of a gas diffused in space would have upon the movements of the planets. From this work I extract an example relating to the application of analysis to the motion of our Earth. According to Laplace, the diminution or augmentation which one may attribute to the duration of our sidereal year 3000 years ago, taking into account the uncertainty of the observations, would be ninety seconds at the maximum (a modification of which, however, there is nothing to demonstrate the reality). Accepting a *reduction* of this amount as real, I inquire what density a gas would need to have, to produce it; and I show that it would suffice if there were one kilogr. of matter in vapour in 700 thousand millions of cubic metres—in other words, that the density would be 0·000, 000, 000, 00143 kilogr. It will be seen that we are far from the reduction to the $\frac{1}{2000}$, and even to the millionth assumed by Mr. Siemens. If, instead of taking account only of the resistance opposed by such a gas to the motion of our planet, we direct our attention to the consequences which its existence would have upon that of our atmosphere, we find that, unless we multiply our 700 thousand millions of cubic metres by 10,000, and reduce the density sought for to 0·000, 000, 000, 000, 0001 kilogr., our atmosphere would be in a few moments *swept away* by the pressure exerted above by the interstellar gas.

M. Faye is perfectly justified in saying that it is not such or such a degree of rarefaction, but that it is the vacuum (*of matter*, of course) that the astronomer requires, to ensure the stability of the movements that his analysis shows. This vacuum no doubt upsets the doctrine, supposed to be so undeniable, which ascribes all the phenomena of the physical world to movements and collisions of material atoms independent of each other. Some day or other, no doubt, this doctrine will have to give up its existence, and its defenders will have to resign themselves to admit in the physical world something more than matter in motion. In a remarkable letter to Bentley, Newton said that one must be destitute of all aptitude for a serious philosophical discussion to suppose that between two bodies which seem to attract each other at an unlimited distance, there is not something which establishes this relation; but, he adds immediately, is this intermediary material or immaterial? This I leave to the reader to decide. With that great genius undoubtedly there was no uncertainty upon this latter point; but, perhaps justly, he refrained from putting before his contemporaries a solution which might have seemed incomprehensible to them, as it still is, apparently, to so many minds of the present day.

On the Conservation of Solar Energy.

A Reply, by C. W. Siemens, to the Note of M. G. A. Hirn, and translated from the Comptes Rendus, *November 27th,* 1882.

M. G. A. Hirn has published in the *Comptes Rendus* of Nov. 6th a communication to the Académie des Sciences concerning my hypothesis regarding the conservation of solar energy, to which I hasten to reply. At the same time I feel some personal embarrassment, since M. Hirn declares his uncompromising antagonism to those physicists who attribute "all the phenomona of the physical world to movements and collisions of material atoms independent of each other"; and considers that "the day will not be long in coming, when physicists will be content to admit something in nature beyond matter in motion."

For my part I must admit that I am an adherent of this materialistic principle, being convinced that it alone can lead us, when supported by experiment, to reliable conclusions regarding the great phenomena of nature.

I shall reply to the physical and mathematical objections of M. Hirn in the order in which they are severally presented.

The French physicists have been the first to throw doubt on the exaggerated estimates of the temperature of the Sun formed by Père Secchi and others, exaggerations that were very common also regarding the fusing points of solids previous to the brilliant researches of Pouillet, H. Sainte-Claire Deville, and others.

M. Hirn estimates this temperature at 20,000°, and very justly concludes that all compound bodies produced during approach will be again completely dissociated in these intensely heated regions, and that this action will absorb all the heat previously developed by combustion. M. Hirn regards this temperature as a minimum, basing his view on the experiments of Professor Langley; but I venture to think that regarding these he cannot be in possession of full information. The instrument employed by Professor Langley, the Bolometer, is a very ingenious development of my electrical pyrometer (*Proc. R. S.* 1871, and *Journal of the Society of Telegraph Engineers*, 1875), which has been frequently employed in metallurgical investigations; I have consequently followed Professor Langley's researches with a very special interest, and on the occasion of his recent visit to Europe I had the opportunity during his stay at my country house of discussing with him questions of solar physics, and have not found that our opinions were very divergent. I have calculated the temperature of the photosphere to be below 3,000°, an estimate based on comparative observations on gas-burners and electric arcs.

The interesting experiments of Professor Tyndall, described in his book on *Radiant Heat* (p. 260), show that a gas-burner, giving an intense light, produces luminous and non-luminous rays in the proportion of 1 to 25, and the temperature of such a burner may be taken at 1,700°. A platinum wire, heated almost to the point of fusion (1,800° according to H. Sainte-Claire Deville) by a galvanic current, emits in luminous rays $\frac{1}{24}$ of the energy imparted to it and $\frac{23}{24}$ in non-luminous rays, while in Tyndall's electric arc produced by 50 Grove's elements $\frac{1}{10}$ of the rays produced were luminous.

Proceeding on these important data I have first reproduced a dynamo-electric current of the strength due to 50 Grove's elements, and have found that Tyndall's arc would be produced by a current of about 5 ampères and 36 volts, giving a light of 20 carcels measured in a horizontal direction. The temperature of an arc of this kind was given by M. Becquerel in 1860 as between 2,070° and 2,100°. An arc produced by a current of 43 ampères and 42 volts according to my own experiments gives 450 carcels; whence it follows that in the latter case $\frac{450}{20} \times \frac{5}{43} \times \frac{36}{42} \times \frac{1}{10} = \frac{1}{4}$ approximately of the total energy appears in the form of luminous rays. The temperature of this arc, following the analogy drawn from other sources of light, cannot exceed 2,500°.

According to the data of Professor Langley, a quarter only of the energy which reaches us from the Sun is luminous (including therein the ultra-violet rays), and admitting that a considerable portion of the latter is absorbed before reaching our atmosphere, it still follows that the temperature of the photosphere cannot much exceed that of our most powerful electric arcs, it may be 2,800°.

The total quantity of radiant energy proceeding from a

given surface is dependent in the first place on the nature of the radiating body. This will be a minimum in the case of a solid body with a smooth surface, and a maximum in a thick mass of incandescent gas, for it is a known fact in physics, and specially confirmed in the case of the photosphere by the researches of Professor Langley, that heat-rays traverse incandescent gas almost without absorption. The prodigious radiation of the photosphere is then a proof of its great thickness, while its temperature can be determined by the proportion of luminous rays which it emits, a proportion not greatly exceeding that which we meet with in our electric arcs. It appears, then, that whatever may be the interior temperature of the Sun, that of the photosphere which surrounds it is not beyond the conditions necessary for combustion, of which the temperature limit is 3,000°, supposing the density equal to that of our atmosphere. But the current does not descend below the photosphere, and it is therefore unnecessary to presume that a second decomposition of the matter combined in the photosphere must take place.

Another objection raised by M. Hirn relates to the transmission of the light of the stars through vast distances, filled, according to my views, with an absorbing medium. It appears to me that the doctrine of the diminution of the intensity of light in proportion to the square of the distance is not applicable without modification to the light of the stars. Professor Langley has proved that a considerable portion of the solar light is lost by absorption before reaching our atmosphere, this being especially the case with the blue rays; further, Mr. J. W. Draper, of New York, has stated in his scientific memoirs, that it is especially the yellow ray which decomposes the carbonic acid and water in the leaf-cells of plants, and my researches on the chemical effect of electric light on vegetation, continued for four years, confirm his observations. On the other hand the diagrams of the solar spectrum[1] by Professor Langley show great gaps, where

[1] See Appendix, pp. 102 and 104.

no effect is produced on the bolometer. May it not be possible that there exist in the luminous spectrum wave-lengths less favourable to the decomposition of certain vapours, and therefore capable of traversing space filled with these rarefied gases to a far greater distance than other rays? Several astronomers have expressed the opinion that besides the visible stars there exist millions of stars of which the light never reaches us, a hypothesis which accords with my view of the existence of a gradually absorbing medium.

The third objection of M. Hirn is based on the mechanical resistance which a material gas diffused through space would offer to the movements of the planets: he shows that to satisfy the sidereal retardation admitted by Laplace of ninety seconds in the last 3,000 years, a degree of rarefaction is necessary such that one kilogram of gas occupies a volume to 700,000,000,000 cubic metres. The learned mathematician does not tell us whether in his calculation he took account of the tangential motion of the planet, or only of the duration of its year. A diminution of tangential velocity would involve a reduction of the mean distance from the Sun, and consequently, following the third law of Kepler, the decrease of velocity would have very little effect on the length of the year.

It would be of interest to know what is the physical law on which M. Hirn has based his calculations of air resistance; the classical researches of Poncelet and others relate almost exclusively to the motion of fluids confined in channels, and are therefore inapplicable, while for the motion of solids through unconstrained fluids we are still in want of a well-founded experimental basis. As far as I know, the only effective experiments on a large scale on the resistance of unconstrained fluids are those undertaken at Torquay by the late Mr. William Froude for the English Admiralty. The striking results at which Mr. Froude arrived are described in a paragraph of his presidential address to the Mechanical Section of the British Association in 1875. He says:—

"The theory of stream lines discloses to us the startling

but true proposition, that a submerged body, if moving at a uniform speed through a perfect fluid, would encounter no resistance whatever. By a perfect fluid, I mean a fluid which is free from viscosity, or quasi-solidity, and in which no friction is caused by the sliding of the particles of the fluid past one another, or past the surface of the body."

He adds:—

"I cannot pretend to frame a list of the many eminent mathematicians who originated or perfected the stream line theory; but I must name from amongst them Professor Rankine, Sir William Thomson, and Professor Stokes, in order to express my personal indebtedness to them for information and explanations, to which chiefly (however imperfectly utilised) I owe such elementary knowledge of the subject as alone I possess."

On the other hand, among the experiments made to determine the resistance of solids wholly immersed in fluids, we have anemometrical experiments, which give by no means concordant results. The English meteorologists, in observing wind-pressure on a surface one foot-square, have deduced a resistance of 61 lbs. (260 kilograms per square metre) for a velocity of 50 metres per second; whereas General Didion, employing discs of one square metre area, has found for the same velocity a total resistance of 194·7 kilograms, or only 40 lbs. per square foot.

Our most eminent mathematicians have maintained hitherto that these discrepancies arise from errors of observation, and that a given wind should produce at least as much pressure per square foot on a large surface as on a small.

An important series of observations has however been made very lately under the direction of Messrs. Fowler and Baker (the well-known engineers of the great projected bridge over the Frith of Forth), the result of which does not accord with that view but is consistent with the theory advanced by Mr. Froude. They have established on a small island in the Frith of Forth three anemometrical plates, the centre one having an area of 27 square metres (12 feet high by 20 feet broad), and those on either side, circular in form, being 1·6 ft. in diameter, equivalent to an area of ·18 square metre. They found that the same wind, normal to the surface, produced a pressure of 15·4 lbs. per square foot (65·1 kilograms per square metre) on the small, and 8·4 lbs. per square foot (35·3 kilograms per square metre) on the large plate.

Following a like proportion, the pressure of the same wind on the surface of an exposed building would probably not exceed 3 lbs. per square foot of surface, a pressure more consistent with facts of observation than that deduced by a calculation based on the uniformity of pressure per unit of surface. Distributed over the enormous surface of a planet the resistance would probably not exceed $\frac{1}{1000}$ part of that deducible from the laws of resistance hitherto assumed by physicists, and based on the idea of actual impact; whereas according to the laws developed by Froude, the resisting elastic fluid (without boundaries) simply performs a lateral oscillation of small intensity in allowing the solid body to pass. The atmosphere of our earth, instead of being swept away, would, according to these views, have the useful effect of filling the space in front and in rear, and of thus acting the part of lubricating matter. Unless all these physical researches are without value, the resistance to the motion of the planets in an elastic and very rare medium must be a mere fraction of the amount hitherto generally accepted.

May I be permitted, before concluding, to recapitulate in favour of my hypothesis the following points already brought forward by me on previous occasions:—the gas contained in meteorites and in the nuclei of comets; the zodiacal light; the equatorial extension observed in America on the occasion of the total eclipse of 1880;[1] the recent spectroscopic researches by Captain Abney, showing the presence of hydrocarbons in space between the solar and terrestrial atmospheres. To these I may add the careful observations on the Sun made by Mr. R. C. Carrington, and described in his work

[1] See p. 91.

Observations on the Spots of the Sun, 1863; Mr. Carrington has established by these important observations that the angular motion of the photosphere is not the same from the equator to the poles. A revolution is completed in 24·9 days at the equator, in 26 at the latitude of 25°, and in 27·4 days at 50° latitude, the retardation in the two hemispheres being almost identical. To what cause should we be able to attribute such a retardation, if it is not to a current of new matter, which, entering at the polar surfaces and receiving the rotatory motion by friction against the penumbra, gives rise in the intermediate zone to great disturbances—the Sun spots? It is probable that such matter, entering the photosphere at the poles, will cause a movement within the solar atmosphere analogous to our terrestrial trade-winds; only it must be remembered that the trade-winds are the result of the solar rays in heating the terrestrial air in the tropics, whereas in the Sun no similar cause of motion exists. It can easily be shown on the contrary that if the Sun rotated with his atmosphere in empty space, the only effect produced would be a moderate accumulation in a direction normal to the axis of rotation; this eccentricity once established, all atmospheric motion in a tangential direction must cease. The polar retardation, then, which is observable in the photosphere, furnishes, I submit, an incontestable proof of a great inflow from without of gaseous matter at the polar surfaces, passing to the equator, and thence into universal space. In the absence of an opposing force, this vast current must expand in the plane of the ecliptic, and become finally part of the interstellar material: centuries may elapse before the same atoms, which thus leave the Sun to-day in a state of combination, will return to him again dissociated by solar radiant energy.

On a Letter of M. Spoerer concerning a Peculiarity of Solar Mechanics.

A Note communicated to the Académie des Sciences by M. Faye, and translated from the Comptes Rendus, *December 4th,* 1882.

The attention of the Academy has recently been specially directed to the physical constitution of the Sun. According to the theory of Dr. Siemens, the Sun is fed by matter which enters at the poles, and having undergone combustion, flows along the surface of the Sun towards the equator, where by centrifugal force it is projected into space away from the Sun.

It would appear that the centrifugal force is not capable of producing such an effect, since solar gravity is 48,000 times as great.[1] If, however, the existence of a surface current from the poles to the equator be assumed, it would afford an explanation of some of the phenomena of the photosphere—for example, the spots. These spots, especially the more remote, would be urged towards the equator, their heliocentric latitude diminishing with the time. The following letter of M. Spoerer bears very directly on this hypothesis, though undoubtedly the learned observer of Potsdam had no idea of testing it, his object being to elucidate a delicate and important point in the theory of Sun spots:—

"Potsdam, *November 27th,* 1882.

"Since my last letter, I have concluded my study on the motion in latitude of the Sun spots, which I had undertaken on the appearance of a work on the subject published by M. de Rico in the *Memorie degli Spettroscopisti italiana* of June, 1882.

---

[1] Unless gravitation towards the centre of the Sun should be almost counterbalanced by the repulsive force which the Sun would exert on matter in a state of extreme tenuity, as is the case with the tails of comets.

"M. de Rico found from observations in the year 1881 that between the parallels of $+15°$ and $-15°$ of heliocentric latitude the majority of the spots were directed towards the equator, whereas the motion in latitude of spots more remote from the equator was towards the poles.

"Carrington had remarked the same, but had found the motion too small to attach any importance to it. For my part I had not concerned myself with the question, as it had appeared to me that these small movements took place indifferently in either direction. I have just resumed my observations of the last twenty years (1861 to 1880) on this subject, and have arrived at the following results :—

"The spots have been divided into two groups :

"1. Those observed during a single rotation.

"2. The spots of longer duration observed during two rotations at least. These latter results have the advantage that they are not sensibly affected by the slight uncertainty regarding the position of the solar equator.

I.

"In the following table I have included only those spots which have changed at least 0°·4 in latitude during $n-2$ days, n being the number of observations on each spot. The sign + indicates increasing latitude, the sign – decreasing latitude, and the number 0 includes those spots which have changed less than 0·4°.

Latitude.	Northern Hemisphere.			Southern Hemisphere.			On both Hemispheres.		
	+	0	–	+	0	–	+	0	–
From 0° to 5°	2	14	4	4	6	2	6	20	6
" 5 " 10	5	34	10	3	22	9	8	56	19
" 10 " 15	4	25	6	9	33	5	13	58	11
" 15 " 20	5	16	5		24	8	5	40	13
" 20 " 25	5	10	2	2	11	1	7	21	3
Above 25		8	2	4	10	4	4	18	6

"From the above table it appears that there is a slight excess of spots between the parallels 5° and 10°, whose motion is towards the equator, and also a slight excess of spots between 20° and 25°, which move towards the poles.

"The following series is rather more decisive.

II.

"Here the minimum displacement is 0°·4 in twenty days, and the sign + and – have the same meaning as before. The sign 0 includes those spots whose motion in latitude has been less than 0°·4 in twenty days. The last column indicates the motion during twenty-seven days of all the spots indifferently.

Latitude.	Northern Hemisphere.			Southern Hemisphere.			On both Hemispheres.			Mean variation for 27 days.
	+	0	−	+	0	−	+	0	−	
From 0° to 5°	0	1	0	3	5	2	3	6	2	0·0
,, 5 ,, 10	2	3	5	2	5	5	4	5	10	−0·28
,, 10 ,, 15	3	10	5	6	1	5	9	11	10	−0·04
,, 15 ,, 20	5	9	3	1	3	1	6	12	4	+0·19
,, 20 ,, 25	7	2	2	1	3	1	8	5	3	+0·63
Above 25	3	1	0	3	2	0	6	3	0	+0·91
TOTALS	20	26	15	16	19	14	36	42	29	

"The mean values given in the last column are for the most part exceedingly small, and their significance depends entirely on the regularity of their increase.

"The numbers themselves in this column are uncertain; but it would be useless to give the probable errors, as their uncertainty is sufficiently shown by comparison with the numbers given in the adjoining columns."

It is apparent that all these observations from Langier and Carrington to M. Spoerer, extending over a great number of years, agree in showing that the displacement of the spots in latitude is either inappreciable or very small, and that the spots remote from the equator tend towards the poles, rather than in the opposite direction.

This result is in direct opposition to the theory, to which I previously alluded. It is, moreover, confirmed by all that we know of the other superficial formations of the Sun, granulations, faculæ, indentations of the chromosphere, protuberances. None of these give evidence of a great current from the poles to the equator. Further, there remains the crucial question, independent of all hypotheses, as to the direction of the currents of the photosphere. I have carefully studied this point, and confining myself exclusively to the spots of long duration, have concluded that they move neither towards the poles nor towards the equator, their small movements in latitude being purely oscillatory and confined within very narrow limits.

In the last very remarkable communication which Dr. Siemens has addressed to us in reply to the objections of M. Hirn, he treats these questions fundamentally. He believes that the increase in angular velocity of successive zones, in proportion to their proximity to the equator, is due to the retarding effect in the polar zones of the influx of matter at the poles, not originally possessing any rotation. This polar current, he says, would give rise in the intermediate zone to those immense whirlpools, the spots.

It is precisely the hypothesis long ago adopted by Sir John Herschel; and I should myself have admitted the same, had I been able to verify by the observations of Langier and Carrington the existence of currents from the poles to the equator. There would be, in fact, a phenomenon analogous to that we are acquainted with in our own atmosphere, where the lower currents flow towards the equator, and the upper currents, which Herschel supposed also to exist in the Sun, from the equator to the poles, forming and carrying with them huge vortices, or cyclones.

But neither Langier nor Carrington nor I have found anything similar in the Sun, and we have just seen that M. Spoerer, during his twenty years' observations, has not discovered the least trace of the movements from the pole to the equator, which Dr. Siemens requires for his theory.

If, then, a retardation of the surface rotation takes place, and the fact is beyond dispute, we must seek the cause, not in a medium exterior to the Sun, as does Dr. Siemens, nor in an inadmissible flattening of his atmosphere, like Sir John Herschel, but in the ascending and descending movements which are continually taking place in the internal mass, and which incessantly bring into contact with the photosphere masses having a smaller linear velocity, and which then participate in the surface radiation, entirely escaping solidification.

On the Conservation of Solar Energy.

A Reply, by M. G. A. Hirn, to the Critical Note addressed to the Académie des Sciences by Mr. C. W. Siemens, and translated from the Comptes Rendus, *December 11th,* 1882.

In the *Comptes Rendus* of November 27th, Mr. Siemens endeavours to answer the various objections I put forward against his new theory on the Conservation of Solar Energy. It is easy to show that the reply of the eminent physicist does not refute my arguments.

1. With regard to the temperature of the photosphere of the Sun, I have relied on what Mr. Langley has published in the *Proceedings of the American Academy of Arts and Sciences*, October 9th, 1878, p. 116.

Having, with the aid of a new and original experimental method compared the radiation of the Sun with that of Bessemer steel in fusion, Mr. Langley has found that for an equal area of radiating surface, the first is eighty-seven times as great as the second; and this number is a minimum. The actual number is necessarily much greater, according to the author himself, if account be taken of the conditions under which the experiment took place. Mr. Langley shows besides that the temperature of this steel, when in fusion, would be nearly 2,000°.

If the description of the experiments of Mr. Langley be carefully followed, and his judicious manner of employing the thermo-electric pile noted, it is easy to see that the expression "magnitude of radiation" does not mean the "quantity of heat" emitted in a given time, but rather the intensity of the heat, or, in other words, the temperature. As all physicists will agree, the researches of Mr. Langley are among the most beautiful on the subject, and in my estimation are decisive in determining the minimum temperature of the Sun, in assuming which at 20,000° I was probably within the actual value.

In support of this I would further put forward an argument of a very different nature. Among the many claims of Mr. Clausius to the gratitude of the scientific world, one of the most prominent is the way in which he has analysed what constitutes the temperature of a body. He shows that a temperature cannot be raised by merely concentrating rays; that if, with a perfect concave mirror, we could gather together all the heat radiated from a body at 100°, for example, a thermometer placed at the focus would not be raised above 100°. I say "above," although in taking account of all the causes of loss which would in this case intervene, it is evident that the 100° would never be reached in reality.

It follows that if, by the aid of concave mirrors and lenses, we could concentrate the solar rays on a very small surface, the temperature indicated by a thermometer placed at the point of concentration would only be a minimum in comparison with the real temperature of the Sun. Experiments which have hitherto been made have shown that in the proportion in which we increase the surface of the lenses and reflectors, the temperature at the focus is raised, and we can only guess a limit to this elevation. Now we know that with the aid of the imperfect lenses at our disposal we can ignite diamond and melt platinum; it is then more than probable that with larger and more perfect reflectors and refractors, such as we could now construct, the effect would be proportionately greater. Accepting, however, what we have found as a limit, and noting that from the nature of the experiment more than $\frac{9}{10}$ of the disposable solar light and heat is lost as far as regards its effect on the thermometer, we still arrive at a number much larger than 2,000° as the real temperature of the Sun.

If, then, the temperature of the Sun cannot be nearly so low as that admitted by Mr. Siemens and others, my first objection remains in its entirety: the chemical compounds supposed to be produced during the approach to the Sun would be again dissociated, and the heat thereby developed would be absorbed in the dissociation.

2. I pass at once to the third objection. In the researches which I have made to determine the various effects which would result from the presence of a material fluid in space, I have had recourse to some special analytical methods which I cannot here explain. I confine myself to saying that in forming the equations of the problem I started from the principles generally admitted in Hydrodynamics, on the validity of which I do not think there can be any serious contest.

A fluid which "offers no resistance to bodies moving in it," certainly does not exist in nature, and can only exist as a mental conception, resting on hypotheses which have not been verified. . . . The combustion of shooting stars, of meteorites, and of ærolites at a height where the density of the air is reduced to one ten-millionth, and perhaps even further than this, show that these bodies experience an enormous resistance on account of their planetary velocity, and there is absolutely no distinction between these phenomena and those we study on the surface of the earth. If there is a part of applied mechanics where the laws determined on a small scale hold in practice on an indefinite scale, it is certainly the branch of Hydrodynamics which has for its object the study of the laws of resistance of an unlimited fluid to the motion of bodies, great or small, which are immersed in it; or inversely, of the pressure exerted by an unlimited fluid in motion on bodies at rest. The degree of precision attainable in ballistic calculations, the exactitude with which it is possible to estimate the mechanical effect of wind on such obstacles as buildings, sails of ships, wind-mills, etc., fully confirm the validity of the principles on which the calculations are founded. Except by inventing new properties of matter, and entering into the region of arbitrary hypothesis, we have no authority whatever for saying that a material fluid extended through space would behave with regard to the planets, comets, and asteroids, otherwise than the air would behave, in a degree proportional to its density, with regard to the bodies, great or small, which move in it, and in particular with regard to these same asteroids in the form of shooting stars, or meteorites. In a word, I maintain the fraction 0·0,000,000,000,000,001 as expressing the density of a material interstellar fluid, whose existence, if supposed real, would render our planetary atmospheres impossible.

On Solar Energy.

Further reply, by C. W. Siemens, to M. Faye and M. Hirn, and published in the Comptes Rendus, *January 2nd*, 1883.

It is with some hesitation that I again venture to address the Académie des Sciences in defence of my hypothesis regarding the conservation of solar energy; I trust, however, that M. Faye and M. Hirn will pardon me for pointing out where they misapprehend, as it appears to me, some of the physical laws and conditions upon which I rely for proof of my views regarding a question which has attracted the attention of physicists in several countries.

M. Faye, in answering Dr. Spoerer (*Comptes Rendus*, 4th December), makes two critical observations regarding my hypothesis, which, if admitted, would destroy its very foundation. He says that the centrifugal force upon the solar equator amounts to only $\frac{1}{48000}$ part of solar gravitation, and that expulsion into space by centrifugal force is out of the question, unless we assume some imaginary expansive force such as appears to be active on the tail of comets. I am anxious to state that I am well aware of the great superiority of solar attraction over centrifugal force at the solar surface (which I had evaluated at $\frac{1}{48800}$); nor do I assume any expansive forces different from what we can verify by experiments in our laboratories.

In order to illustrate perhaps more clearly than I have hitherto done the cause of the powerful outflowing current which I regard as a necessary consequence of fluid material, however attenuated, filling stellar space, I will suppose the existence of a bent tube (similar to that referred to by Newton in his *Principia*) passing from the solar centre in the equatorial and the polar direction respectively, both branches extending to an immaterial but equal distance into space. The effect of solar gravitation on the matter contained within the two branches of this tube, would be to cause the same density in both at equal distances (the temperatures being equal), according to the law of Mariotte. At any distance, R, from the centre, an increment of, say, a centimetre in length in one branch, would be precisely balanced by a similar increment at the distance, R, in the other branch. If now the equatorial arm of the tube was made to partake of the solar rotation, the equilibrium of pressures towards the centre would be immediately disturbed, the two increments at the distance, R, would no longer balance, but the one in the equatorial direction would move outwards, causing that in the polar direction to move inwards; the places that had been occupied by this matter would be immediately taken up by similar matter within the tubes, and the same want of equilibrium would be immediately applicable to these similar volumes of fresh matter, causing them to move a further step in the same direction. The same disturbing cause of equilibrium being applicable continually and for every value of R, *and the stellar material beyond the tube having free access to the same*, it follows that a current must be established passing towards the Sun in the polar and from the Sun in the equatorial arm of the tube.

Solar gravitation determines the density of the gaseous columns within the two arms of the tube equally without impeding their flow; on the contrary, the greater the density due to solar gravitation, the greater will be the effect of rotation upon the gaseous column, and the more determinedly will the current flow through the hypothetical tube. I need hardly add that what is proved for the confined area within such a tube must be true also for all free matter, extending from the Sun into space in the radial and equatorial directions, and the amount of matter thus circulating has to be estimated by the two factors—its tangential velocity at the solar equator, and the vast superficial area of the equatorial region. In flowing outward this current would expand into larger and larger sectional areas, causing its onward velocity, in reaching stellar density, to diminish, whereby its kinetic energy will be converted into potential energy or pressure, before mingling with the great interstellar ocean of gaseous matter through which our whole Solar System is supposed to move. This potential energy or pressure, affecting matter in space, serves to generate, by gradual acceleration, the polar current, in the manner illustrated by the hypothetical bent tube.

The power necessary to maintain this current must be derived from solar rotation, but considering that the matter arrives at the surface of the Sun with a certain velocity, the Sun has only to supply as much rotatory energy as is necessary to effect a change of direction, and to make up for intermolecular friction. As regards this mechanical action, the second law of Thermodynamics (as developed chiefly by Clausius and Rankine) applies, that is to say, a certain amount of solar heat must descend from a higher to a lower potential; but inasmuch as the mechanical power required to maintain the current is small in comparison with the chemical work performed in dissociation (and to which the second law of Thermodynamics does not apply), the cooling effect involved must also be relatively small, and this loss of heat may possibly be replaced by solar shrinkage (the enormous value of which has been demonstrated by Helmholtz), by the falling into the Sun of planetary matter as suggested by Mayer, Waterston, and by convection currents from the interior of the Sun, as suggested by Sir William Thomson. It may be interesting to observe that the supposed mechanical action of the Sun is accomplished with the least possible expenditure of solar heat, because the range of absolute temperatures, T—T°, upon which the economy of every caloric engine depends, amounts in the case of the Sun, to say 2930° Centigrade, as contrasted with 160°, the greatest working range of temperature obtainable in a steam-engine.

M. Faye, referring to the researches of Dr. Spoerer, and to his own important investigations regarding the irregular deviations in heliocentric latitude of Sun spots, points out that Sir John Herschel was mistaken in ascribing the existence of those spots to a solar equatorial current due to polar flattening of the solar atmosphere. I accept M. Faye's view that the polar depression of the Sun being very slight, no appreciable equatorial current could be ascribed to it; but I venture to think that if Sir John Herschel had imagined the existence of a polar current of light material, taking its origin outside the solar atmosphere, his deductions regarding the cause of Sun spots would have been consistent with the facts of observation.

We have on our earth analogous conditions to those which my hypothesis supposes to exist on the Sun (but in the inverse order), in the form of a heated and expanded equatorial current. The equatorial or trade-wind current gives rise in our latitude to those cyclones, the approach of which on western shores is very frequently communicated to us by the Atlantic telegraph. These cyclonic currents pass across the Atlantic, sometimes with a southern and at others with a northern deviation; but they necessarily follow in the main, and in obedience to the laws of gyration, an easterly course, and if they could be seen from a point in space would appear to pass around the earth in about twenty-three hours and forty minutes. The supposed solar current in passing from the poles towards the equator would cause cyclones showing an acceleration in the opposite sense, that is to say, would effect a solar revolution in say twenty-seven instead of twenty-five terrestrial days. Their deviations in heliocentric latitude would be influenced on the one hand by the generating current forcing them towards the equator, and on the other hand by their own vortex action in the dense metallic vapour of the Sun forcing them towards the pole. I shall be required, no doubt, to furnish an explanation of this latter action, which I attribute to the circumstance that a cyclone occupying say 1° in 30° latitude would in advancing latitudinally have less matter to displace on the side towards the pole, where the solar diameter is inferior, than on that towards the equator, where the solar diameter is superior. Having less mass to move in the smaller circle facing the pole, it will encounter less resistance in that direction and will therefore verge towards the pole. The relative importance of the two forces would be determined by the depth to which the cyclone is rooted in the inferior metallic vapour, or the size of the spot, and by its angular distance from the pole. This vortex pressure would increase necessarily with the degree of solar latitude, and we should thus find a rational explanation of Dr. Spoerer's important observations, to the effect that the spots of high latitude tend towards the pole, while those of the equatorial regions verge more frequently towards the equator. It would be important to know whether in the same latitude the deeply rooted or larger spots do not more frequently verge towards the pole, and the smaller or superficial ones towards the equator.

If the observed retardation of the solar photosphere were due to the sudden transportation of matter from an inferior to a superior radius of the Sun's body, the retarding effect thus produced could certainly not be less near the equator than near the pole, and there would apparently be no reason why Sun spots should be seen any less at the pole or the equator itself than within the two intermediate regions. If we may suppose the lower atmosphere of the Sun to consist of comparatively dense metallic gases at a high temperature, cyclonic action would have the effect of drawing photospheric matter into the vortex funnel; here solar dissociation, alluded to by M. Hirn, would undoubtedly take place, giving rise in the first place to a local depression of temperature—the appearance of darkness—and in the next to explosive action caused by a temporary release from pressure at great solar depth. Streams of vivid light must also appear on the dark background, whenever the dissociated matter again reached a sufficient elevation to admit of recombustion. Thus far, then, I am disposed to agree with M. Hirn, that redissociation upon the solar surface may actually take place, but the ultimate heating effect due to an inflowing and outflowing current such as I suppose, must be determined by the chemical condition of that current on entering and leaving the solar photosphere, *the intermediate changes being capable of producing local disturbances without affecting the final balance of cause and effect.*

M. Hirn formulates his objection to the working of my hypothesis under two distinct heads (*Comptes Rendus,* December 11th), to which I venture to make the following reply. Regarding the temperature of the solar photosphere, I admire with him the ingenuity and value of Mr. Langley's investigation "On the Temperature of the Sun" as recorded in the *Proceedings of the American Academy of Arts and Sciences,* for May 1879, though I must differ from him as regards some of the conclusions which he draws from Mr. Langley's investigation. I fully accept Mr. Langley's conclusion to the effect "that the determinations of M. Violle placing the temperature of the photosphere at 1500° C. are evidently considerably too low, and that it is demonstrably over 1800° C. and may be considerably above that temperature;"[1] nor do I disagree with Mr. Langley when he states that the solar heat radiation must be as a minimum something like 100 times greater than that from melted platinum, seeing that he guards himself against being understood to say, that this greater radiation proves any particular temperature in excess of the 1800° C., which latter he adopts indeed as his minimum. In his quantitative experiment a smooth surface of fluid metal is compared with the gaseous photosphere, and no allowance is made for the important factor, m, in Dulong and Petit's formula; nor does Mr. Langley attempt to establish a ratio of dependence of radiation with increase of temperature. I may here remark that the solar

[1] M. Violle, in a letter addressed to the Académie des Sciences, and which appeared in the *Comptes Rendus* of 22 January, 1883, admits that the temperature of the solar photosphere must exceed 1800°, and accepts my estimate making it nearly 3000° Centigrade.

temperature of 2800° C. at which I arrived by a different process of reasoning is just 1000° C. above Mr. Langley's minimum—a difference quite sufficient I consider to harmonise his observations as regards amount of radiation with my own. The opinion on this question of Sir William Thomson, must be deemed of great interest by all physicists; in a paper communicated by him quite recently to the Philosophical Society of Glasgow on Photometric Measurement, he says: "In the year 1878 Rosetti reckoned the solar temperature to be about 9000°, but possibly the most probable value yet assigned was that of C. Wm. Siemens, about 3000° Centigrade."

When M. Hirn, referring to the investigation of Clausius, says that the temperature of a focus of light or heat can never exceed that of the surface, whence the radiant energy is derived, I am fully prepared to agree with him. It is evident that the temperature produced in the focus of a good parabolic reflector directed towards the solar disc cannot exceed the solar temperature, but I venture to maintain that it can be made to approach that temperature much more nearly than M. Hirn seems prepared to admit; if the reflector is carefully made, of sufficient size, and placed upon a considerable elevation. The question is one which has particularly attracted my attention, and a few years ago I mounted a heliostat, with a carefully silvered parabolic reflector of 18 centimetres diameter, at my country house near Tunbridge Wells, which is situated about 160 metres above sea level. The principal object I had in view was to ascertain whether dissociation could be produced within the focus. The temperature produced was such that the point of a rod of carbon pushed through a hole at the apex of the parabolic reflector became vividly luminous when reaching the focus but not more so than it would have been in an electric arc of small power. One of the experiments I made consisted in directing an ordinary gas flame through the focus, with the result that the solar rays were sufficient to retard, without suspending, the gaseous combustion; the effect produced was similar indeed to that observed in the Regenerative Gas (or Siemens) furnace, when employed for the production of mild steel, or fused iron (*fer fondu*). In this furnace the metal attains approximately the same temperature as in the Bessemer Converter, whereas the portion of the furnace above the metallic bath is at a considerably higher temperature, since the heat of the flame is communicated to the metal through a certain thickness of scoria. It is interesting to observe that when this furnace is at its highest heat, the flame has a decidedly bluish appearance, and the rate of combustion is considerably retarded by what constitutes a partial dissociation. The sides of the furnace (of pure silica) attain necessarily almost the same temperature as the flame, yet in first opening the furnace door, and thereupon shutting off the gas supply, an extraordinary decrease of radiant energy is at once perceptible, showing that the gaseous incandescent atmosphere is far superior to the solid refractory substance of the sides in heat radiating power.

The only means by which I have succeeded in obtaining calorific effects exceeding those of the regenerative gas furnace have been by the use of my electric furnace, which M. Dumas saw at the Electrical Exhibition at Paris, and thought sufficiently interesting to make mention of before the Academy. In employing a current ranging between 250 and 300 ampères, I succeeded in melting 4 kilogrammes of platinum in 15 minutes, commencing with a cold crucible, and being desirous of carrying out some further experiments in electric fusion, I induced my friend Professor Huntington to join me in a series of researches, the results of which were communicated to the Chemical Section of the British Association at Southampton in August last, and published in *The Engineer* of the 8th September, 1882, a reprint from which I enclose herewith.[1]

The difficulty that presented itself in the practical application of this furnace for metallurgical purposes, was principally due to the circumstance, that during fusion a considerable

[1] See Appendix, p. 91.

portion of the material or metal under treatment assumed the gaseous condition, and issued from the close chamber of the furnace with considerable force through the smallest crevices. Thus in one experiment a weight of 340 grammes of copper was treated for about half an hour, when, at the end of that time, only 21 grammes remained in the crucible, the remainder filling the apartment in the form of a thick and not readily condensible vapour. The furnace temperature was practically limited in these experiments by the point, at which even the most refractory materials, such as Tungsten, assumed the gaseous condition, and considering that evaporation of the metals took place before their fusion was accomplished, I conclude that their evaporative point is not much above their fusing point.

Regarding the frictional resistance of an attenuated medium, M. Hirn thinks it necessary to adhere to the extraordinary admissible degree of tenuity of 0·0,000,000,000,000,001 kilogramme mentioned in his previous communication. Even this degree of attenuation might suffice for my purpose if it was taken to apply to a distance from the Sun equal to that of Neptune or Uranus; but I hope that further evidence will be produced to establish my deductions to the effect that planetary resistance, if calculated upon the formulæ now generally applied to ballistic problems, would enormously exceed the actual resistance in a free medium. Mr. Froude did not deny, nor do I in any way overlook, the great frictional resistance which must be encountered by a projectile of comparatively small dimensions in passing through the air, or by a meteorolite passing through the confines of our atmosphere, with a velocity greatly accelerated by terrestrial attraction during its approach; but both the stream-line theory of Froude, and my own observations regarding anemometer plates of large and small areas, go to prove that the resistance of a comparatively large body or surface encountering a free medium increases much more nearly proportionately to its circumferential development than to its area. I may add, that the further observations reported to Messrs. Fowler and Baker from the Frith of Forth, confirm those I mentioned in my last communication, and I hope soon to be in a position to bring forward additional proof in support of my views, by means of an apparatus now in course of construction.

Observations on the last Communication of Dr. Siemens on Solar Energy: by M. Faye.

Communicated to the Académie des Sciences, and translated from the Comptes Rendus, *January 8th,* 1883.

When Mr. Siemens, who has been signally successful in treating electrical forces and high temperatures, refers to his experiments, the reader cannot but derive much advantage by studying his communications; but when he discusses the physical constitution of the Sun, we encounter much which is hard to admit.

Thus I raised the objection that the equatorial centrifugal force of the Sun is far too weak in comparison with solar gravity to allow the Sun to project into space, the particles arriving at the equator.

Mr. Siemens answers me by referring to the hypothetical bent tube, to which Newton had recourse in discussing the flattening of the poles of our globe, the tube having one branch along the line of the poles, and the other directed towards any point on the equator. But Newton made the two branches of the tube emerge on the same surface of the planet, whereas Mr. Siemens supposes, in the case of the Sun, a bent tube with indefinite branches extending into cosmical space. When he impresses on the equatorial branch of this tube the rotation of the Sun, it is certain that the centrifugal force at the extremity would increase indefinitely in proportion to the length of the tube, whereas, gravity at the extremity will diminish more rapidly still, in the inverse ratio of the square of the length. Consequently, the equilibrium will be destroyed, the matter will flow out from the extremity of the tube and form a sort of equatorial current, while cosmical matter will be drawn into the immovable polar branch. If necessary, Mr. Siemens would make all the gas, with which he fills the universe, pass in this way through his tube.

But the learned author has not remarked in applying this action to the Sun, that he supposes the Sun has communicated his rotation to the indefinitely extended medium, which according to the hypothesis surrounds him. This medium would revolve, as if rigidly connected with the Sun, which Mr. Siemens certainly has not in view; on further reflection I believe that he will find some difficulty on this point.[1]

On two Objections of Professor Young, of New Jersey, against the Cyclonic Theory of Sun Spots: by M. Faye.

A Communication to the Académie des Sciences, and Translated from the Comptes Rendus, *December 26th*, 1882.[2]

In Simon Newcomb's *Popular Astronomy*, Mr. Young, whose beautiful spectroscopic researches on the sun are well known, refers to this theory in the following words: "The theory of M. Faye appears to me, on the whole, to be the most reasonable of all which have been put forward, but it is difficult to reconcile it with the want of visible traces of rotation in the majority of the spots." Quite recently, in a work on the Sun, which has just been published in the International Library of M. Alglave, Mr. Young again raised this objection, and points out a second difficulty which appears to him decisive. It is known that the successive zones of the photosphere have not the same angular velocity. It is to these differences of velocity that

[1] It will be seen from my previous communication regarding the solar fan action that it does not depend on the rotation of the gaseous matter filling space. This matter would enter the polar branch of the hypothetical tube irrespective of any initial motion of the arm, and would be delivered equatorially with the motion imparted to it by the tube. C. W. S.

[2] This communication of M. Faye on the nature of Sun spots corroborates in many remarkable points the views expressed by the author in his final reply to MM. Faye and Hirn. M. Faye's Note, though preceding the author's Letter in date of publication, appeared after the latter had been despatched.

I attribute the formation of the solar cyclones or spots. On the other hand, Mr. Young, availing himself of the formula I have given for the diurnal velocity in any heliocentric latitude l, viz.:

$$862' - 186' \text{ Sin}^2 \text{ l.}$$

finds that the variation from l=20° to l=20°. 1′ is only 4 ⅛ miles per day, while the distance between the two parallels is 123 miles. This appears to him to be insufficient to give rise to cyclones in the Sun.

I appreciate these objections, but believe them to be anticipated. Cyclones have been taken to imply violent vortices; and it has been imagined that, if the spots of the Sun are cyclones, the edges should be violently torn and distorted; the whole should revolve rapidly about the centre, the luminous filaments of the penumbra would be twisted into spirals, etc. If such is necessarily the case, I would at once admit that the appearance of the spots is by no means cyclonic, and that a velocity of 4·1 miles, per day, at a radius of 123 miles, only representing an angular velocity of 2° per day at the edge of the vortex, does not at all correspond to this view.

But I hope that Mr. Young will be impressed by the simple remark I am about to make on this subject.

The upper part of the diagram represents a vertical section of a terrestrial tornado; the lower part represents an ordinary Sun spot with the serrated edge of the photosphere, the grey penumbra, the dark nucleus, and the entirely black centre discovered by the Rev. Mr. Dawes, with the exception of some details, physical rather than geometrical. The two figures are the vertical and horizontal sections of one and the same object; viz. a vortex about a vertical axis. We see the terrestrial vortices from the first point of view, quite low down, almost at the foot of the vortex, where the motion is very violent, while the upper opening is hidden by clouds. On the other hand we see the solar vortices from above, from the second point of view, showing the vortex projected on the surface of the Sun; the edge of the vast upper opening being alone visible to us. There, contrary to the lower part, which we do not see on the Sun, the velocity of rotation is very slow.[1]

What we see on the Sun, we should see also on the earth, could we raise ourselves high above the earth and contemplate from a height a horizontal projection of the cyclone or tornado in full action, making a vast opening in the midst

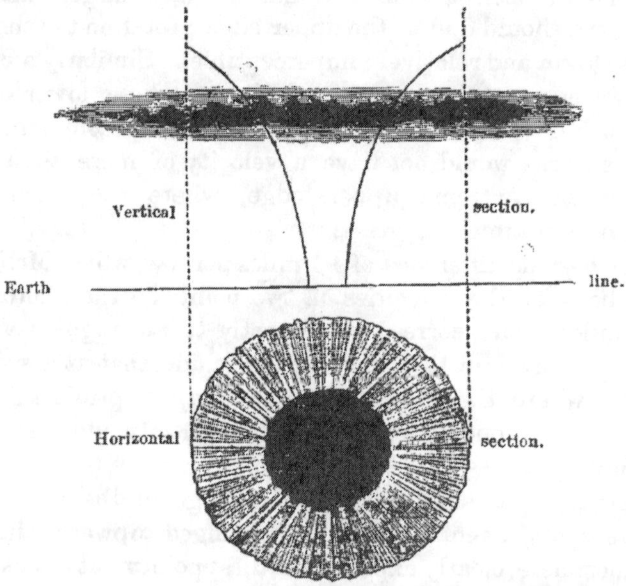

of our aërial current charged with cirrus. If we were at a sufficient distance, we should see hardly any rotation at the edge, or at least, a very long time must elapse before it

[1] I know nothing more striking than this simple geometrical identity of two phenomena so different in appearance, viz. the Sun spots and terrestrial cyclones. Since the nucleus of the solar cyclone is black, the matter which moves in it is cold, consequently the vortex motion is downwards. Since terrestrial mechanics ought not to differ from solar mechanics, the vortex motion is also downwards in terrestrial cyclones, a conclusion which I have verified with regard to our cyclones, waterspouts, and tornadoes.

became very distinct. As to the dark centre of the cyclone, we should see nothing of the enormous rotation there taking place.

Almost the only law of Hydrodynamics, relating to vortices, is that the angular velocity in a well-established vortex varies from one point to another inversely as the square of the distance from the axis. Further, if we examined a water-spout having a base a few metres in diameter, and stretching upwards to the clouds, which obscure the mouth of the funnel—an opening many hundred times larger than the base—we should find at the upper edge a rotation ten thousand times slower and relatively imperceptible. Similarly a cyclone or a waterspout, the angular velocity of whose lower edge is 180° per day, which is quite possible at the commencement of a tempest, would not have a velocity of more than 2° per day at the extreme upper edge, where the diameter is perhaps ten times as great.

Further, the difference of 4·1 miles per day, which Mr. Young finds between the velocities of two points on the photosphere 123 miles apart, corresponds exactly to an angular velocity of 2° per day, and this does not preclude that at a sufficient depth; where the diameter of this imperceptible solar pore is reduced to one mile, the angular velocity will be 30,000° per day.

This slowness of rotation at the edge of the vast funnel of the spots, even when it is prolonged upwards into the chromosphere, clearly explains the disappointment of observers, who complain that they very rarely find any traces of rotation. Such traces would only be visible at the edges, for in the centre, where the rotation is more rapid, there is only the dark and cold gas, which is being rapidly engulfed in the dark hole, discovered by Dawes, corresponding precisely to the constricted part of the funnel of our aërial vortices.

If the luminous clouds detached from the edges could continue to shine in the cold centre, we should certainly see them following the current in descending spirals. But they are rapidly enveloped in the cold hydrogen flowing in from above, and die away not far from the edge. In the penumbra it would be useless to seek for traces of rotation. It is no more a part of the vortex than the envelope of clouds which surrounds our waterspouts and tornadoes, and renders their contour visible. It is composed of luminous clouds resembling those of the photosphere, but much rarer. They originate in the tranquil space situated above the funnel, on account of a local depression of temperature; and the penumbra so formed ends abruptly, irregularly bounding the nucleus, properly so called, because nearer the axis the ascending currents, loaded with the vapour which gives rise to these clouds, are thrust aside by the gas which is set free, and mounts from the lower end of the cyclone. The gyratory motion only encroaches on this envelope in case of segmentation. The luminous threads are then twisted locally in various directions, as shown in the beautiful diagrams of Mr. Langley.

It is in this way (and it is necessary to insist on it) that the clouds enveloping waterspouts and tornadoes do not in general give any indication of the violent vortex which they surround. It is true that justly celebrated meteorologists have long denied the internal rotation of tornadoes because there are no indications of it on the outlines; hence, in order to convince them, it is necessary to seek traces on the earth in the position of overturned trees and in the debris of our houses. I have myself undertaken a discussion of this subject before the Académie.

Briefly here is my reply to the objections of Mr. Young, which at first sight appear so plausible :—

1. The inequality of velocity (for which my formula gives only a mean value, the accuracy of which is impaired by the presence of the spots) between the parallel lines of the currents of the photosphere, and without doubt, also of the chromosphere, is amply sufficient to give rise on the Sun to vortices of every size from the largest spots, which would easily engulf our earth, down to the scarcely visible pores.

2. If in general no traces of rotation are visible at the

edge of the spots, it is on account of the slowness of rotation there. They would not, moreover, be found in our cyclones if viewed from above on the edges of their extended openings.

But, although we seldom meet with the indications sought by Mr. Young, which in fact ought generally to be absent, it is easy to find other very characteristic indications, which are by no means accidental, but occur in every spot. I have long ago pointed these out, and will now simply enumerate them. They are the distinctive characteristics of all gyratory motion, and are found both in the Sun, and in our own atmosphere.

1°. The circular form assumed by all the spots in their earliest stages.

2°. The extended conical form of their mouth.

3°. The marked constriction which this form undergoes at a lower level, made especially evident in the black hole of Dawes.

4°. Their tendency to enlarge, while almost always keeping their circular form.

5°. Their tendency to break into segments, which, starting with a certain degree of development, form partial spots. These in their turn, as soon as they have differentiated themselves, and a narrow band of the photosphere has been established between them and the ascending currents of the interior, form complete spots with penumbra—nucleus and the black hole of Dawes more or less concentrically placed. This phenomenon is so frequent and striking in our own cyclones, that meteorologists have adopted the same word, "segmentation," to distinguish it.

6°. Their regular course following the line of the current which has originated them.

7°. Their long duration, comparable and often superior to that of our cyclones, which extend over entire weeks, while describing their enormous trajectories on our globe. This long duration is compatible only with gyration round a vertical axis.

8°. Their mode of disappearance depending on their

mechanical action. This action has the effect of absorbing the inequalities in the velocities of the surface currents, which are drawn below, and having performed their peculiar work disappear. When in this way a more uniform region is momentarily established in a stream of water or gas, the vortex ceases to be fed; and rapidly contracts and disappears.

9°. The reappearance around the spots (or the pores) of the hydrogen, which has been engulfed by them, and which, set free at a certain depth, rapidly remounts around the vortex to the point whence it came, and even shoots beyond by reason of its acquired velocity. Hence the production of faculæ, the appearance of the erruptive protuberances, and the extraordinary vertical circulation of the hydrogen, which takes place incessantly between the chromosphere and lower strata, and *vice versâ*. This is the only phenomenon which is peculiar to solar vortices.

I have proved, and meteorologists are beginning to believe, that the terrestrial vortices formed round a vertical axis have their origin in the upper currents of our atmosphere; thence they descend to the earth, where they expend the energy they have acquired above and concentrated in transmitting it downwards. It is interesting to recognize on the Sun this law of terrestrial mechanics even to the minutest details. The identity established between the spots of the Sun and our cyclones furnishes the key of these mysterious phenomena; and when, in passing from the earth to the Sun, we see these phenomena successively projected on a vertical and then on a horizontal plane, we are in a better position to form a more complete idea of both.[1]

[1] It appears from this interesting communication that M. Faye attributes the Sun spots to similar causes to those which I have assumed in my last answer to him, the important difference between us being that M. Faye supposes the generating currents to proceed from the interior whereas I suppose them to come from sources exterior to the sun. The question being thus narrowed it will most likely be determined absolutely before long by independent observers. C. W. S.

APPENDIX.

APPENDIX.

ON THE ELECTRIC FURNACE.[1]

By C. W. SIEMENS, D.C.L., F.R.S., *and* A. K. HUNTINGTON,
Professor of Metallurgy, King's College, London.

THE electric furnace has previously been described in the *Journal of the Society of Telegraph Engineers*, June 1880. It has since been found advisable to surround the furnace with a coil. By this means the direction of the arc can be regulated at will, and the tendency which it has to fly to the sides of the crucible be checked.

The furnace consists of a crucible, *a*, of any convenient size, in the bottom of which is pierced a hole to receive the positive electrode, *c*, the negative electrode, *d*, which passes through a hole in the lid of the crucible, being suspended from one end of a beam, the other end of which is attached to a hollow cylinder of soft iron, *e*, free to move vertically within a solenoid coil of wire. The force with which the cylinder is drawn into the coil can be counterpoised by a sliding weight, *g*, on the beam. One end of the solenoid coil is connected with the positive, and the other with the negative pole. The coil having a high resistance, its attractive force on the cylinder is proportional to the electromotive force between the electrodes, *i.e.* to the resistance of the arc. The length of the arc is therefore regulated automatically. This is a point of great importance, as, were it not so, the resistance of the arc would rapidly diminish as the temperature of the atmosphere within the crucible increased, and the result would be that heat would be developed in the dynamo machine. The extinction of the arc by sudden change in its resistance or by the sinking of the material in the crucible is thus also avoided. The crucible is surrounded with some infusible substance, *b*, which is also a bad conductor of heat. Gas retort carbon or sand answers

[1] Read before Section B of the British Association at Southampton, 1882.

well for the purpose. The electrodes may be of such carbon as is used in electric lighting or of any other convenient conducting substance. They may, if desired, be cooled by circulating water through or round them, or by exposing them as far as possible to the air. For example, in one experiment a half-inch nickel positive pole was employed, the lower end being inserted into a solid rod of copper about one inch square by six inches long. With this pole, no other means of keeping it cool being adopted, one pound of grain nickel was fused in a clay crucible and poured in eight minutes, starting with all cold. The electrode was but little attacked, and no leakage occurred.

There are two great advantages possessed by the electric furnace, viz. that the temperature attainable is practically only limited by the refractoriness of the materials of which the furnace is constructed, and that the heat is developed immediately in the material to be fused, instead of first having to pass through the containing vessel. The temperature to be obtained by the use of fuel is limited by dissociation. Deville has shown that carbonic acid undergoes dissociation at the ordinary atmospheric pressure at about 2600°. C.

In the experiments made by the authors, five D 2 machines driven by a Marshall's twelve-horse power engine were employed; one being used as an exciter. The current ranged between 250 and 300 ampères. The most refractory clay crucibles supplied by the Patent Plumbago Crucible Company were invariably cut through in a few minutes, and, except for experiments of short duration, were useless. Plumbago crucibles stood exceedingly well. Obviously, however, they could not be employed for all purposes, owing to their tendency to cause carburisation of the metal experimented with. In some experiments the fusion of metal was effected in a bed of lime, sand, or electric light carbon dust. The latter is a very bad conductor, and, as in the case of lime and sand, allows the arc when once formed to maintain a passage through it to the metal beneath.

Wrought Iron.—Six pounds of wrought iron were kept under the action of the arc for twenty minutes and the metal then poured into a mould. It was found to be crystalline, and could not be forged. This is the result which has always been obtained when iron, nickel, or cobalt have been fused. Although the remedy, viz. the addition of a little manganese just before pouring, is well known, the cause remains still unexplained.

Steel.—As much as twenty pounds of steel files have been melted in one charge, the time required being about one hour, starting with the furnace hot. With such large quantities the metal has invariably been full of blowholes.

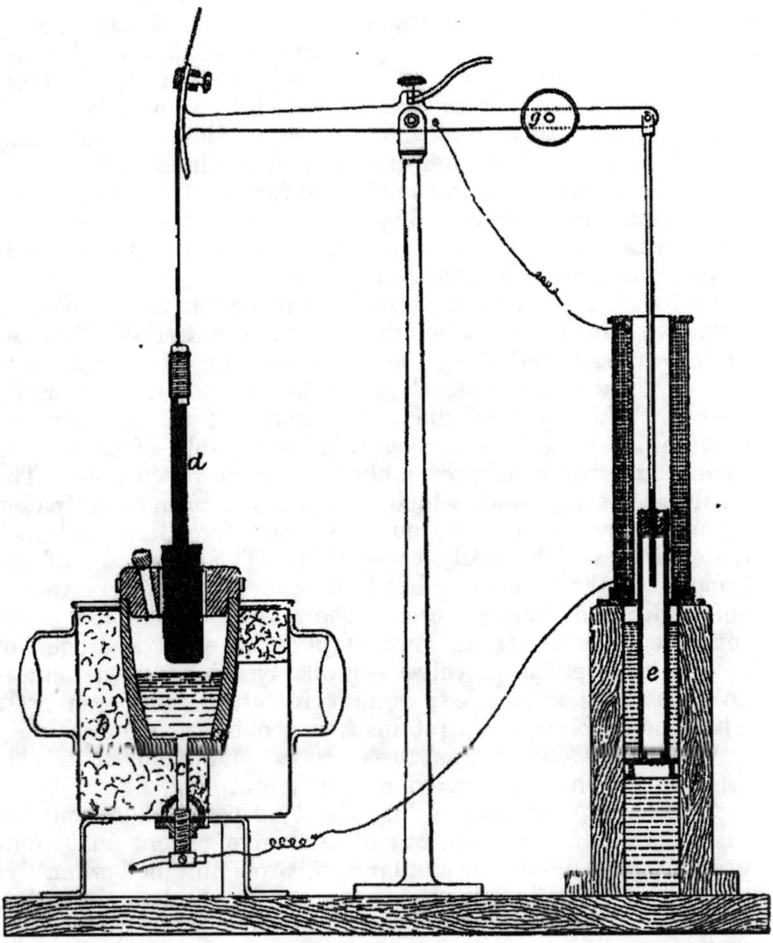

White iron, fused in a clay crucible for thirty minutes, when fractured did not appear to have undergone any change. White iron and coke were introduced into the furnace; the resultant metal was slightly grayer than the original. When, however, retort carbon was substituted for the coke a good gray iron, soft and easily workable, was readily obtained in fifteen minutes, starting with the crucible hot. On another occasion, starting all cold, at the end of thirty minutes the metal, although it had been well fused, had not been rendered grayer. The difference between these two results was possibly due to the temperature being somewhat higher in the one case than in the other. This is a point of considerable practical interest. Four pounds of white iron, fused with carbon dust for three-quarters of an hour, yielded a very gray crystalline iron. In another experiment, in which eight ounces of gray iron, produced in the electric furnace from white iron, were re-melted in carbon dust for ten minutes a very gray metal was obtained, from which on slow cooling a large quantity of graphite separated.

Cast iron, fused and kept under the action of the arc for forty-five minutes in carbon dust was not materially changed as to grayness, and the general character of the metal as to the way in which it worked under the tool was not materially altered. The object of the experiment was to ascertain the maximum amount of carbon iron is capable of taking up under circumstances presumably the most favourable. The result is hardly that which would have been anticipated. Some of the same cast iron was fused for fifteen minutes under lime, which nearly covered it. The character of the fracture of the metal was but little altered by this treatment, when slight differences, due to the rate of cooling, are taken into account. A strong smell of phosphoretted hydrogen or of a phosphite was perceived—probably the latter. This was only observed in the experiment in which lime was used. The lime employed still retains a very offensive odour.

When *spiegeleisen* was fused in a plumbago or a clay crucible graphite separated as the metal cooled.

Siliceous pig iron, containing about 10 per cent. silicon, was fused by itself, it showed but little change, except that some graphite separated. A similar result was obtained when five pounds of the siliceous pig were fused for one hour in carbon dust. On fracturing the ingot obtained, a large quantity of scales of graphite was found in a hollow which traversed nearly the whole length of the ingot at its centre. The fracture of the metal was still that so characteristic of highly siliceous iron, and was practically the same as that of the original pig iron.

A series of experiments was made to determine the maximum amount of carbon pig iron is capable of taking up in the presence of a given quantity of silicon. Gray cast iron and pig iron containing 10 per cent. of silicon were fused together in carbon dust, the ratio between them being varied so as to yield metal with from ¼ per cent. to 9 per cent. of silicon.

A similar series was made, only substituting sulphur for silicon. No odour of sulphurous acid was perceived; therefore, presumably, no sulphur was volatilised. This is somewhat remarkable, considering the nature of the experiment. It was thought that investigations of this kind might have an important practical as well as more purely scientific interest—admitting, for the sake of argument, that any such distinction really exists—in assisting to determine the conditions in the blast furnace, &c.

Nickel.—A positive pole of this metal—cast malleable by Wiggin & Co.'s process [1]—half inch in diameter, was passed through a hole in the bottom of a clay crucible. A carbon negative pole was used, but soon after the commencement of the experiment a deposit of nickel formed on the end of it, so that practically it was a nickel pole. This deposition of metal on the negative pole was also observed with some other metals—notably with tungsten. Whilst disclaiming any special knowledge on the point, Professor Huntington suggested whether this phenomenon—which is the reverse of that generally recognised as taking place—might not depend on the relative volatility of the matter composing the poles. In the furnace arranged as just described, one pound of grain nickel was fused and poured in eight minutes. The fused metal had a brilliant granular fracture. It could not be cut properly in the shaping machine, shearing off under the tool. One pound of grain nickel fused in carbon dust for twenty-five minutes yielded a dark gray carburised metal, which worked well under the tool. On another occasion an equal quantity of nickel, similarly treated, gave a "blowy" metal, which could not be worked. Some carburised nickel, made as described above, was fused in a clay crucible for twelve minutes, and allowed to cool gradually in the furnace; the fracture became whiter, and the grain closer.

Copper.—Three quarters of a pound of copper were fused for about half an hour in carbon dust. On examining the result, it was found that all but about three quarters of an

[1] See paper on "Nickel and Cobalt," by A. K. Huntington, in July number of the *Journal of the Society of Chemical Industry*.

ounce had been vapourised. Those who were present during the experiments suffered no ill effects from the atmosphere charged with copper, which they must have breathed.

Platinum.—Eight pounds of platinum were rendered perfectly liquid in about a quarter of an hour.

Tungsten.—Half a pound of tungsten in powder was subjected to the action of the arc in a clay crucible. Dense fumes were evolved, a cavity about one and a half inches across the top being formed. The furnace was allowed to cool down slowly. When the crucible was removed, it was found to have been very much attacked below the point to which the arc extended. The inference is that the crucible had been attacked by the metal at the temperature of the experiment. The metal was fused only to an inappreciable depth beneath the cavity formed by the arc. The unfused metal underneath was covered with very beautiful iridescent crystals of tungsten, which under the microscope appeared to be well-formed prisms. They have not yet been measured. The crystals had evidently been formed by the slow cooling of the vapour distilled down from the surface.

A very large number of experiments was made with tungsten, the results of which showed that it could not be fused, except in very small quantities at a time. It was possible to build up a small ingot by fusing a little of the tungsten, and then adding little by little gradually. Even then the pieces obtained were for the most part spongy and unsatisfactory. The best results arrived at were when tungsten which had already been fused was employed in the building-up process. Once the metal had been fused, it did not fume much in melting, doubtless owing to the greatly reduced surface exposed.

Tungsten fused in the electric furnace is, when untarnished, pure white, and brittle, the grain being very close. Tungsten hitherto has only been obtained as a gray powder, by reducing the oxide with carbon or hydrogen, or in minute globules in the ordinary small electric arc. Tungsten has its fusing point lowered by the addition to it of carbon. Under these conditions a solid piece of moderate size can, without much difficulty, be obtained. From 1000 grains of powder fused in carbon dust 650 grains were recovered, the remainder having been volatilised, and from 450 grains of the fused metal 410 grains were obtained on refusion. One piece of tungsten which had been treated under the conditions most likely to cause it to be highly carburised was analysed. It contained 1·8 per cent. of carbon. The metal was very white, close in grain, and brittle.

From the foregoing experiments it is clear that the amount of any given metal which can be successfully fused in the electric furnace, and the time required in effecting the fusion, are dependent on (*a*) the relation between the volatilising point and the fusing point, *i.e.* the extent to which the volatilising point is higher than the fusing point; (*b*) the conductivity of the metal for heat.

It thus happens that platinum can be more readily melted than steel, and in greater quantity for a given expenditure of energy. This inference is believed by Professor Huntington to be justified by the observations and experiments so far made.

It still remains to examine chemically the specimens referred to in this paper.

In the discussion on the communication made by Professor Huntington, Dr. Siemens remarked that the limit of the temperature producible by means of the electric furnace is as yet unknown, for although the resistance of the arc would probably increase with temperature, that in itself would only cause a further development of heat. The results obtained with copper, although apparently pointing to a drawback in the use of the furnace for melting purposes, yet might prove of importance in dealing with metals in the vaporous condition. He could not agree with Professor Huntington's suggestion as to the cause of the deposition of metal on the negative pole. He thought it was due to the negative pole being much cooler than the positive.

Dr. Gladstone inquired whether the deposit was crystalline or in fused globules.

Professor Huntington replied that it was in the latter condition.

Mr. Terrill (Swansea), remarked that the loss of copper by volatilisation in smelting was much greater than it was generally supposed. During an accidental escape of sulphuretted hydrogen in the works he had observed a thick deposit of sulphide of copper extending over a large area. He had detected copper deposited even on the zinc counter of the refreshment bar at the railway station some distance from the works. The discussion was continued by Mr. Maxwell Lyte, Prof. Vernon Harcourt, and the president, Prof. Liveing, who thought that such experiments as had been made might be of great service in the study of metals.

SUNLIGHT AND SKYLIGHT AT HIGH ALTITUDES.

An Abstract of a Paper by CAPTAIN ABNEY, F.R.S., *read before Section A of the Meeting of the British Association at Southampton,* 1882 ; *together with a Report of the Remarks made by* PROFESSOR LANGLEY *in the subsequent Discussion.*[1]

AT the Southampton meeting of the British Association, Captain Abney read a paper in which he called attention to the fact that photographs taken at high altitudes show skies that are nearly black by comparison with bright objects projected against them, and he went on to show that the higher above the sea-level the observer went, the darker the sky really is and the fainter the spectrum. In fact, the latter shows but little more than a band in the violet and ultra-violet at a height of 8,500 feet, whilst at sea-level it shows nearly the whole photographic spectrum. The only reason of this must be particles of some reflecting matter from which sunlight is reflected. The author refers this to "water-stuff" of which nine-tenths is left behind at the altitude at which he worked. He then showed that the brightness of the ultra-violet of direct sunlight increased enormously the higher the observer went, but only to a certain point, for the spectrum suddenly terminated at about 2,940 wave-length. This abrupt absorption was due to extra atmospheric causes and perhaps to space.. The increase in brightness of the ultra-violet was such that the usually invisible rays L, M, N, could be distinctly seen showing that the visibility of these rays depended on the intensity of the radiation. The red and ultra-red part of the spectrum was also considered. He showed that the absorption lines were present in undiminished force and number at this high altitude, thus placing their origin to extra atmospheric causes. The absorption from atmospheric causes of radiant energy in these parts he showed was due to "water-stuff," which he hesitated to call aqueous vapour, since the banded spectrum

[1] Printed in *Nature*, October 12th, 1882.

of water was present, and not lines. The B and A line he also stated could not be claimed as telluric lines, much less as due to aqueous vapour, but must originate between the Sun and our atmosphere. The author finally confirmed the presence of benzene and ethyl in the same region. He had found their presence indicated in the spectrum at sea-level, and found their absorption lines with undiminished intensity at 8,500 feet. *Thus without much doubt hydrocarbons must exist between our atmosphere and the Sun, and it may be in space.*

Prof. Langley, following Capt. Abney observed: The very remarkable paper just read by Captain Abney has already brought information, upon some points which the one I am about, by the courtesy of the Association, to present, leaves in doubt. It will be understood then that the references here are to his published memoirs only, and not to what we have just heard.

The solar spectrum is so commonly supposed to have been mapped with completeness, that the statement that much more than one half its extent is not only unmapped but nearly unknown, may excite surprise. This statement is, however, I think, quite within the truth, as to that almost unexplored region discovered by the elder Herschel, which lying below the red and invisible to the eye, is so compressed by the prism, that though its aggregate heat effects have been studied through the thermopile, it is only by the recent researches of Captain Abney that we have any certain knowledge of the lines of absorption there, even in part. Though the last named investigator has extended our knowledge of it to a point much beyond the lowest visible ray, there yet remains a still remoter region, more extensive than the whole visible spectrum, the study of which has been entered on at Alleghany, by means of the linear bolometer.

The whole spectrum, visible and invisible, is powerfully affected by the selective absorption of our atmosphere, and that of the Sun; and we must first observe that could we get outside our earth's atmospheric shell, we should see a second and very different spectrum, and could we afterwards remove the solar atmosphere also, we should have yet a third, different from either. The charts exhibited show :—

1st. The distribution of the solar energy as we receive it, at the earth's surface, throughout the entire invisible as well as visible portion, both on the prismatic and normal scales. This is what I have principally to speak of now, but this whole first research is but incidental to others upon the spectra before any absorption, which though incomplete, I wish briefly to allude to later. The other curves then indicate.

2nd. The distribution of energy before absorption by our own atmosphere.

3rd. This distribution at the photosphere of the Sun.

The extent of the field, newly studied, is shown by this drawing (chart exhibited). Between H in the extreme violet, and A in the furthest red, lies the visible spectrum, with which we are familiar, its length being about 4,000 of Ångstrom's units. If then, 4,000 represent the length of the visible spectrum, the chart shows that the region below extends through 24,000 more, and so much of this as lies below wave-length, 12,000, I think, is now mapped for the first time.

We have to $\lambda = 12{,}000$, relatively complete photographs, published by Captain Abney, but except some very slight indications by Lamansky, Desains, and Mouton, no further guide.

Deviations being proportionate to abscissae, and measured solar energies to ordinates, we have here (1) the distribution of energy in the prismatic and (2) its distribution in the normal spectrum. The total energy is in each case proportionate to the area of the curve, (the two very dissimilar curves inclosing the same area,) and on each, if the total energy be roughly divided into four parts, one of these will correspond to the visible, and three to the invisible or ultra-red part. The total energy at the ultra-violet end is so small then as to be here altogether negligible.

We observe that (owing to the distortion introduced by the prism) the maximum ordinate representing the heat in the prismatic spectrum is, as observed by Tyndall, below the red, while upon the normal scale the maximum ordinate is found in the orange.

I would next ask your attention to the fact that in either spectrum, below $\lambda = 12{,}000$ are most extraordinary depressions and interruptions of the energy, to which, as will be seen, the visible spectrum offers no parallel. As to the agent producing these great gaps, which so strikingly interrupt the continuity of the curve, and as you see, in one place, cut it completely in two, I have as yet obtained no conclusive evidence. Knowing the great absorption of water vapour in this lowest region, as we already do, from the observations of Tyndall, it would, *a priori*, seem not unreasonable to look to it as the cause. On the other hand, when I have continued observations from noon to sunset, making successive measures of each ordinate, as the sinking Sun sent its rays through greater depths of absorbing atmosphere; I have not found these gaps increasing, as much as they apparently should, if due to a terrestrial cause, and so far as this evidence goes, they might be rather thought to be solar. But my own means of investigation are not so well adapted to decide this important point, as those of photography, to which we may yet be indebted for our final conclusion.

I am led from a study of Captain Abney's photographs of the region between $\lambda = 8{,}000$ and $\lambda = 12{,}000$, to think that these gaps are produced by the aggregation of finer lines, which can best be discriminated by the camera, an instrument, which, where it can be used at all, is far more sensitive than the bolometer; while the latter, I think, has on the other hand some advantage in affording direct and trustworthy measures of the amount of energy inhering in each ray.

One reason why the extent of this great region has been so singularly under-estimated, is the deceptively small space into which it appears to be compressed by the distortion of the prism. To discriminate between these crowded rays I have been driven to the invention of a special instrument. The bolometer, which I have here, is an instrument depending upon principles which I need not explain at length, since all present may be presumed to be familiar with the success which has before attended their application in another field, in the hands of the President of this Association, Dr. Siemens.

I may remark, however, that this special construction has involved very considerable difficulties and long labour. For the instrument here shown, platinum has been rolled by Messrs. Tiffany, of New York, into sheets, which, as determined by the kindness of Professor Rood, reach the surprising tenuity of less than $\frac{1}{25000}$ of an English inch (I have also iron rolled to $\frac{1}{15000}$ inch), and from this platinum a strip is cut $\frac{1}{125}$ of an inch wide. This minute strip, forming one arm of a Wheatstone's bridge, and thus perfectly shielded from air currents, is accurately centred by means of a compound microscope, in this truly turned cylinder, and the cylinder itself is exactly directed by the arms of this Y.

The attached galvanometer responds readily to changes of

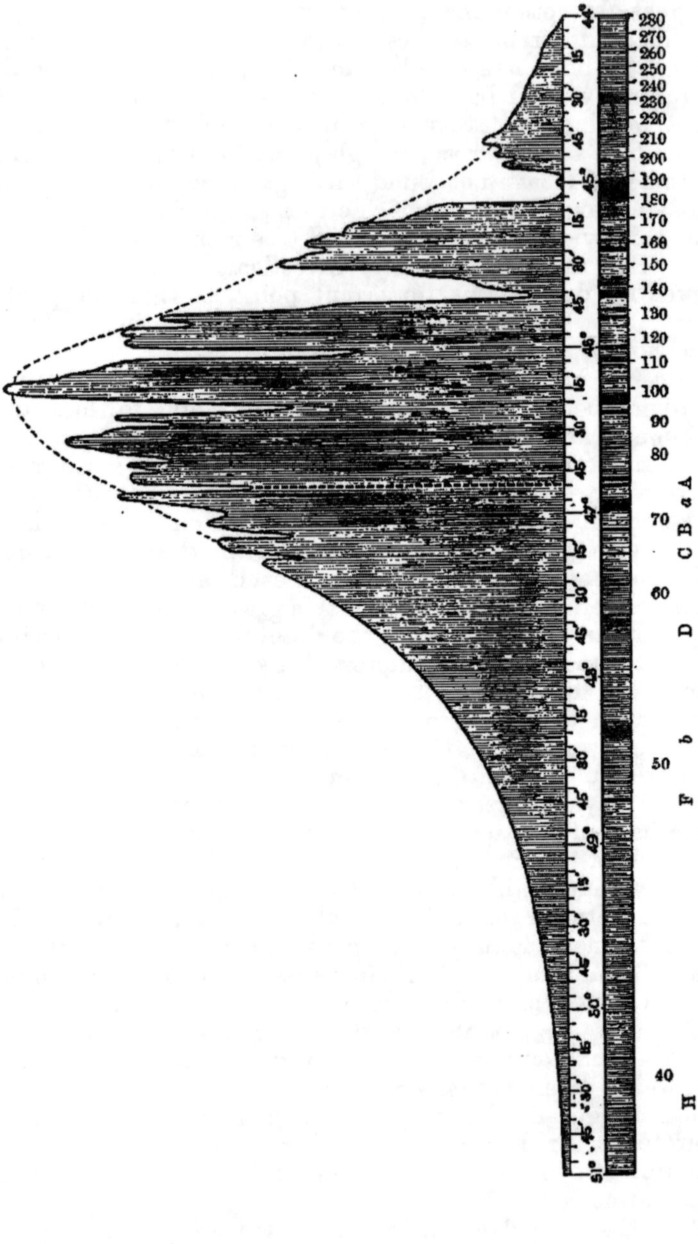

Prismatic Spectrum.

temperature, of much less than $\frac{1}{10000}$° Fah. Since it is one and the same solar energy, whose manifestations we call "light" or "heat," according to the medium which interprets them, what is "light" to the eye is "heat" to the bolometer, and what is seen as a dark line by the eye is felt as a cold line by the sentient instrument. Accordingly if lines analogous to the dark "Fraunhofer lines" exist in this invisible region, they will appear (if I may so speak), to the bolometer as cold bands, and this hair-like strip of platina is moved along in the invisible part of the spectrum, till the galvanometer indicates the all but infinitesimal change of temperature caused by its contact with such a "cold band." The whole work, it will be seen, is necessarily very slow; it is in fact a long groping in the dark, and it demands extreme patience. A portion of its results are now before you.

The most tedious part of the whole process, has been the determination of the wave-lengths. It will be remembered that we have (except through the work of Captain Abney, already cited, and perhaps of M. Mouton), no direct knowledge of the wave-lengths in the infra-red prismatic spectrum, but have hitherto inferred them from formulas like the well-known one of Cauchy's, all which known to me appear to be here found erroneous by the test of direct experiment; at least in the case of the prism actually employed.

I have been greatly aided in this part of the work by the remarkable concave gratings lately constructed by Professor Rowland of Baltimore, one of which I have the pleasure of showing you.

The spectra formed by this, fall upon a screen in which is a fine slit, only permitting nearly homogeneous rays to pass, and these, which may contain the rays of as many as four overlapping spectra, are next passed through a rock-salt or glass prism placed with its refracting edge parallel to the grating lines. This sorts out the different narrow spectral images, without danger of overlapping, and after their passage through the prism we find them again and fix their position by means of the bolometer, which for this purpose is attached to a special kind of spectrometer, where its platinum thread replaces the reticule of the ordinary telescope. This is very difficult work, especially in the lowermost spectrum, where I have spent over two weeks of consecutive labour, in fixing a single wave-length.

The final result is I think worth the trouble, however, for as you see here, we are now able to fix with approximate

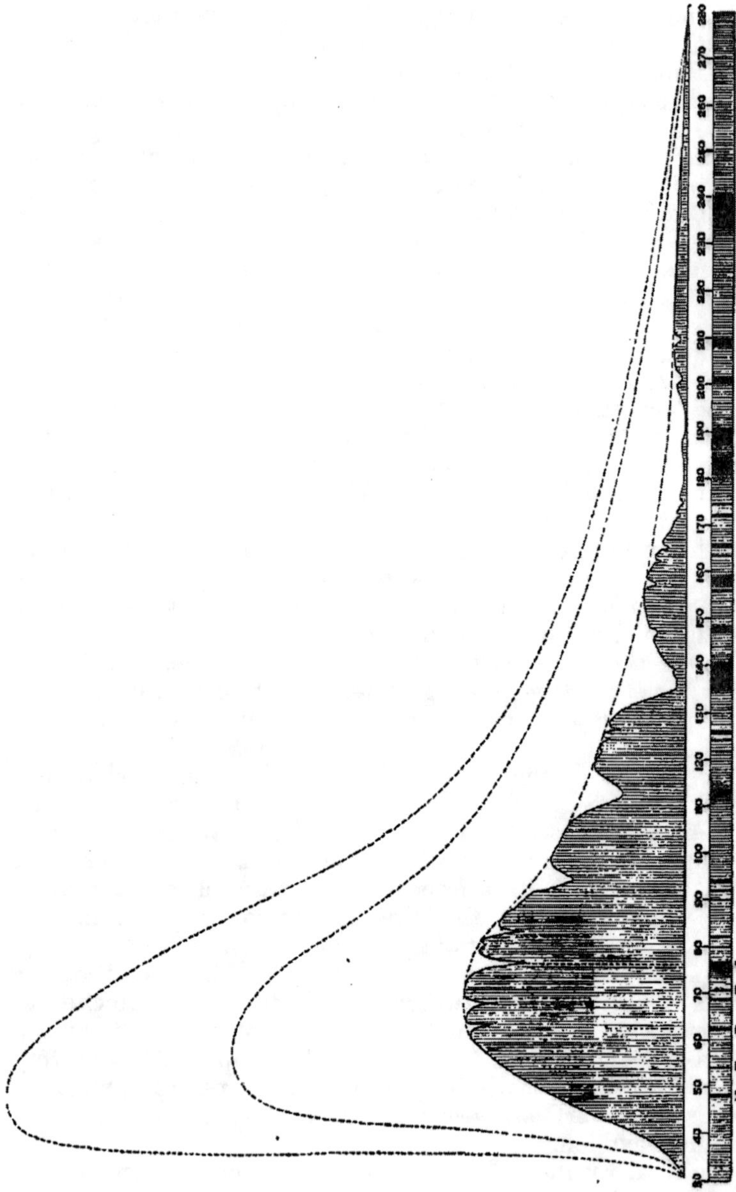

Normal Spectrum (at sea-level).

precision, and by direct experiment, the wave-length of every prismatic spectral ray. The terminal ray of the solar spectrum, whose presence has been certainly felt by the bolometer, has a wave-length of about 28,000 (or is nearly two octaves below the "great A" of Fraunhofer).

So far it appears only that we have been measuring *heat*, but I have called the curve that of solar "energy," because by a series of independent investigations, not here given, the selective absorption of the silver, the speculum-metal, the glass and the lamp-black (the latter used on the bolometer-strip), forming the agents of investigation, has been separately allowed for. My study of lamp-black absorption, I should add in qualification, is not quite complete, I have found it quite transparent to certain infra-red rays, and it is very possible that there may be some faint radiations yet to be discovered even below those here indicated.

In view of the increased attention that is doubtless soon to be given to this most interesting but strangely neglected region, and which by photography and other methods, is certain to be fully mapped hereafter, I can but consider this present work less as a survey than as a sketch of this great new field, and it is as such only that I here present it.

All that has preceded is subordinate to the main research, on which I have occupied the past two years at Alleghany, in comparing the spectra of the Sun at high and low altitudes, but which I must here touch upon briefly. By the generosity of a friend of the Alleghany Observatory, and by the aid of General Hazen, Chief Signal Officer of the United States Army, I was enabled last year to organise an expedition to Mount Whitney in South Califorina, where the most important of these latter observations were repeated at an altitude of 13,000 feet. Upon my return I made a special investigation upon the selective absorption of the Sun's atmosphere, with results which I can now only allude to.

By such observations, but by methods too elaborate for present description, we can pass from the curve of energy actually observed, to that which would be seen, if the observer were stationed wholly above the earth's atmosphere, and freed from the effect of its absorption.

The salient and remarkable result is the growth of the blue end of the spectrum, and I would remark that while it has been long known from the researches of Lockyer, Crova, and others, that certain rays of short wave-length were more absorbed than those of long, that these charts show *how much* separate each ray of the spectrum has grown, and bring, what seems to me, conclusive evidence of the shifting of the point of maximum energy without the atmosphere towards the blue. Contrary to the accepted belief, it appears here also that the absorption on the whole grows less and less, to the extreme infra-red extremity; and on the other hand, that the energy before absorption was so enormously greater in the blue and violet, that the Sun must have a decidedly bluish tint to the naked eye, if we could rise above the earth's atmosphere to view it.

But even were we placed outside the earth's atmosphere, that surrounding the Sun itself would still remain, and exert absorption. By special methods, not here detailed, we have at Alleghany, compared the absorption, at various depths, of the Sun's own atmosphere for each spectral ray, and are hence enabled to show, with approximate truth, I think for the first time, the original distribution of energy throughout the visible and invisible spectrum, at the fount of that energy, in the Sun itself. There is a surprising similarity you will notice, in the character of the solar and telluric absorptions, and one which we could hardly have anticipated *a priori*.

Here too, violet has been absorbed enormously more than the green, and the green than the red, and so on, the difference being so great, that if we were to calculate the thickness of the solar atmosphere on the hypothesis of a uniform transmission, we should obtain a very thick atmosphere, from the rate of absorption in the infra-red alone, and a very thin one from that in the violet alone.

But the main result, seems to be still this, that as we have seen in the earth's atmosphere, so we see in the Sun's, an enormous and progressive increase of the energy towards the shorter wave-lengths. This conclusion, which I may be permitted to remark, I anticipated in a communication published in the *Comptes Rendus* of the Institute of France as long since as 1875, is now fully confirmed, and I may mention that it is so also by direct photometric methods, not here given.

If then we ask how the solar photosphere would appear to the eye, could we see it without absorption, these figures appear to show conclusively that it would be *blue*. Not to rely on any assumption, however, we have by various methods at Alleghany, reproduced this colour.

Thus (to indicate roughly the principle used), taking three Maxwell's discs, a red, green, and blue, so as to reproduce white, we note the three corresponding ordinates at the earth's surface spectrum, and comparing these with the same ordinates in the curve giving the energy at the solar surface; we re-arrange the discs, so as to give the proportion of red, green, and blue, which would be seen *there*, and obtain by their revolution a tint which must approximately represent that at the photosphere, and which is most similar to that of a blue near Fraunhofer's "F."

The conclusion then is, that while all radiations emanate from the solar surface, including red and infra-red, in greater degree than we receive them, that the blue end is so enormously greater in proportion, that the proper colour of the Sun, as seen at the photosphere, is blue—not only "bluish," but positively and distinctly blue; a statement which I have not ventured to make from any conjecture, or on any less cause than on the sole ground of long continued experiments, which, commenced some seven years since, have within the past two years irresistibly tended to the present conclusion.

The mass of observations on which it rests must be reserved for more detailed publication elsewhere, at present I can only thank the Association for the courtesy which has given me the much prized opportunity of laying before them this indication of methods and results.

DISSOCIATION OF ATTENUATED COMPOUND GASES.

By Professor G. D. Liveing, M.A., F.R.S., F.C.S.

Excerpt from the Address to the Chemical Section of the British Association at Southampton in 1882.

I cannot dismiss the subject of chemical dynamics without alluding to the ingenious theory by which the President of the Association has proposed to account for the conservation of solar energy. He supposes planetary space to be pervaded by an atmosphere which, except where it is condensed by the attraction of the Sun and planets, is in a highly attenuated state. The Sun and planets communicate some of their own motion of rotation to the atmosphere condensed about them, and he supposes that in this way an action like that of a blowing fan is set up, by which the equatorial part of the Sun's atmosphere acquires such a velocity as to stream out to distances beyond the earth's orbit, while an equal quantity of gas is drawn in at the poles to maintain equilibrium. The gases thus driven to a distance in planetary space will of course be enormously expanded and highly attenuated, and in this state Dr. Siemens thinks that such of them as are compound may be decomposed by absorbing the solar radiation, and thus the kinetic energy of the Sun's rays be converted into the potential energy of chemical separation. The separated elements, or partial compounds, will in the circulation produced by the fanlike action of the solar rotation be carried back to the polar regions of the Sun as fuel to maintain his temperature by condensation and re-combination. I will not discuss the mechanical part of this theory further than to remark that the fanlike action can only be carried on at the expense of the energy of the Sun's rotation, which must in consequence be continually diminishing, and must in time become too slow to produce any sensible projection of the atmosphere into distant regions of planetary space. As to the chemical side of the theory, Dr. Siemens supposes the gases which pervade the planetary space to be not only of the same kind as the components of our own atmosphere, which on the kinetic theory of gases must diffuse through that space, but also such gases as are not found in our air, but are found occluded in meteorites, which may be supposed to have acquired them in their previous wanderings. Amongst these he specially mentions hydrocarbons which form the self-luminous part of most comets. It is to these gases, together with aqueous vapour and carbonic acid, that he ascribes the principal part in the conservation of solar energy. That compound gases at the extremely low pressure of the planetary space are decomposed by solar radiation is not inconsistent with the laws of dissociation, for it is quite possible that some compounds may be decomposed at ordinary temperatures by mere reduction of pressure, and the radiation absorbed will be the more effective because it will directly affect the vibratory motion within the molecule, and may well produce chemical decomposition before it can, when the free path of the molecules is so much increased by the attenuation of the gas, assume the form of an increased temperature. Dr. Siemens, moreover, adduces a remarkable experiment in confirmation of this supposition. We know, too, the power which our atmosphere, and especially the water vapour in it, has of absorbing the infra-red rays, and that amongst the Fraunhofer lines some of the strongest groups are due to aqueous vapour; and the capital observation made by the spectroscopic observers at the last total eclipse, that the group of lines known as "B," which is one of those produced by aqueous vapour, is greatly strengthened when the Sun's light passes by the edge of the moon and so through the lunar atmosphere, may be taken as a confirmation of the theory that gases like our atmosphere are diffused through space and concentrated about the planets. But if it be true that the compounds are decomposed by absorbing the Sun's rays, we ought to find in our atmosphere the products of decomposition, we ought to find in it free hydrogen, carbonic oxide, and acetylene or some other hydrocarbons. The hydrogen, from its small specific gravity, would not be concentrated in the lower regions of our atmosphere in the same proportions as the denser gases, but carbonic oxide and hydrocarbons could not fail to be detected in the air if they formed any sensible proportion of the gases in the planetary space. That a large portion of solar radiation is intercepted before it reaches the earth is no doubt true, for there are not only the dark bands which are increased by our atmosphere and may reasonably be attributed to the action of like gases pervading planetary space, but there is a continuous absorption of the ultra-violet spectrum beyond the line U, and Cornu has found that this absorption is not sensibly affected by our atmosphere, so that the substance, whatever it be that produces it, may be an agent in the process imagined by Dr. Siemens, but cannot be the means of restoring to the sun any portion of his radiant energy which reaches our distance from him.

Dr. Siemens explains the self-luminous character of comets by the theory that the streams of meteoric stones of which they are supposed to consist bring from stellar space hydrocarbon and other gases occluded within them, and that in consequence of the rise of temperature due to the frictional resistance of such a divided mass moving with enormous velocity, aided by attractive condensation, the occluded gases will be driven out and burnt, the flame giving rise to the original light emitted by the nucleus. Now the spectrum of most comets shows only the principal bands of a Bunsen burner, and is therefore adequately explained by the flame of gas containing hydrocarbons such as have been found in meteorites; but Dr. Huggins has observed in the spectrum of more than one comet, not only hydrocarbon, but cyanogen bands; and, although carbon and nitrogen combine readily in the electric arc, a coal-gas flame in air shows no trace of the spectrum of cyanogen, and it would certainly put some strain on our credulity if it were asserted that cyanogen was one of the gases brought ready-formed by meteorites from stellar space. Dewar and I have, however, recently shown that if nitrogen already in combination, as, for instance, ammonia, be brought into a hydrocarbon flame, cyanogen is produced in sufficient amount to give in a photograph (though not so as to be directly visible) the characteristic spectrum of cyanogen as it appears in the comet. It is therefore no longer necessary to make any other supposition to account for the cyanogen bands in the spectra of comets, than that ammonia, or some such compound of nitrogen, is present as well as hydrocarbons in a state of ignition.

Quite recently Dr. Huggins has observed that the principal comet of this year has a spectrum of an entirely different character, but he is not yet able to say to what elements or compounds it is probably due. The notion that comets may bring us news of distant parts of stellar space, towards which our system is driving, where the atmosphere is not like ours —oxygen and nitrogen—but hydrogen and hydrocarbons, may fascinate the fancy, but the laws of occlusion oblige us to think that the meteorites have not merely wandered through an attenuated atmosphere of hydrogen and hydrocarbons, but have cooled in a much denser atmosphere of those substances, which we can only conceive as concentrated by the presence of a star or some large aggregation of matter. They may, perchance, have come from some nebulous mass, for Draper and Huggins tell us that in the great nebula in Orion hydrogen is dense enough and hot enough to show some of its characteristic lines, besides the F line which is seen in other nebulæ, and is the last to disappear by reduction of density. No comet on visiting our system a second time can repeat the exclusion of its occluded gases unless its store has been replenished in the interval. Tacchini has recently observed that Encke's comet, which is one of short period that does not travel beyond the limits of our system, shows the usual spectrum of three bands. If this observation should be confirmed it will be very difficult to account for the replenishment of its occluded gases. But Encke's comet is a very small object, and one cannot feel very certain about its spectrum, and it will be interesting to see, when Halley's comet next returns, whether it shines only by reflected light or gives us, like so many others, the banded spectrum of hydrocarbons.

THE END.